Bereavement Ministry &
Support Groups

PT 470
AICHP
Dec 31
AH 2842/DC42

Guiding People Through Grief

How to Start and Lead
Bereavement Support Groups

William G. Hoy

Compass Press
Dallas

Manufactured in the United States of America

ISBN 978-0-9677235-4-9

This publication is designed to provide accurate and authoritative advice in regard to the subject matter covered. Even though it is based on the author's experience and knowledge, this book should not be considered as a substitute for professional advice on your situation. If expert assistance is required, the services of a competent professional person should be sought.

❧ Table of Contents ❦

Seven. Help—My Group is Sinking!. 81

Poor marketing ✦ Ineffective leadership ✦ Difficult group members ✦ Exhausted leaders

Epilogue. 89

Resources. 91

Sample promotional flyer ✦ Group handouts on journal-keeping, managing anger, parenting children, and many more

Reading and Internet Resources. 99

General bereavement ✦ Stories to read with children ✦ Helping children and teens ✦ Child and pregnancy loss ✦ Pastoral care in bereavement ✦ Group leadership strategies ✦ Websittes and organizations of interest

Introduction

Becky had just turned 44 when her husband of 22 years was killed in a car crash. In the early months of Becky's grief, she saw an individual therapist. Throughout the process, however, she declared that she *would* not and *could* not consider attending a support group. Her grief was just too different, she explained, and she was not much of a "group person" anyway.

The therapist who worked with Becky, told her about a new support group especially designed for widows younger than 50 who were raising children alone. Becky approached the first group meeting with dread. Once there, however, she connected with four other ladies whose husbands had also died, leaving them as single moms.

Later, she would explain that participating in that group became the strategic turning point in her grief. "Suddenly," she explained, "I realized that others had experienced what I was going through and that they had survived. Knowing someone else made it through made me start believing for the first time that I would, too."

A trained volunteer from a local bereavement center led the group Becky attended. Thousands of groups like this begin every year. Some, of course never seem to get off the ground while others continue—with new faces—for many years.

You may have a lot in common with the person who began Becky's group, and this handbook was written for you. The focus of this handbook is a particular kind of lay volunteer or professional caregiver, one who senses a need and even a "call" to work with bereaved people. You may be planning to begin a new group or you may simply be looking for fresh ideas for the one you now lead. Either way, you will find help here.

"Suddenly, I realized that others had experienced this—and survived; that made me start believing I would, too."

Who Should Use This Handbook

Guiding People Through Grief was designed with several audiences in focus. For lay volunteers and graduate interns, this may be the first support group you have ever led. Even though you are supervised by an experienced professional, you might be searching for ideas about the basics of running a grief group.

If you are a professional therapist with an established practice, you may be considering a grief group as a way to enhance the effectiveness of your work with some of your clients and make a positive contribution to your community. Even if you are fairly new to the concept of a bereavement support group, however, you will discover practical ideas here.

These ideas have been proven through years of experience with a diversity of grief groups

Or, you may work in a profession where support of bereaved people is a part of your work but not your principal focus. Pastors, senior center social workers, and school counselors are included in this crowd. Because bereavement and loss are not your main function, you need quick, easily-applicable ideas for supporting people after a death. You will find help here, too.

The ideas in this handbook are based on the best principles for supporting bereaved persons. Though you will not find this to be a research-laden textbook on bereavement theory, the ideas have been proven through years of experience.

What is in this Handbook?

What you will find here are simple, practical, proven ideas for enhancing group leadership. This handbook is not intended to be the final word on group work with grieving people. *Guiding People Through Grief* includes wide margins to write and make the ideas your own.

I have chosen to write to you in the first person, even though I know this technique drives the editors crazy. Perhaps you will see this handbook as a conversation between us, much like if we were sitting in a room together talking about how to help people in grief. I hope this informality will not be an annoyance to you.

Throughout the handbook, you will find *For Reflection* activities, designed to get you thinking deeply about some aspect of the material you are reading. These activities also make great discussion starters if you are using this handbook to train potential group leaders.

Chapter 1 summarizes the question of why grief groups are helpful in the lives of grieving people and you will discover some ways to increase their effectiveness. Chapter 2 overviews the bereavement process and explains why grief groups help people walk through the experience. Of course, grief is a holistic experience—involving emotional, physical, spiritual, social, and mental processes. So here, you will learn some practical strategies for helping your group talk about every facet of the process.

The "nuts and bolts" of starting groups are addressed in Chapter 3. Ideas for determining how long groups should run, how to screen participants, and how to manage the other logistical details like meeting place and meeting length are all covered here. Chapter 4 answers the question, "What do you do in a grief group?" In addition to discussing ground rules for groups, the chapter equips leaders with the most important skill for facilitating a grief group: asking good questions.

Whether you are leading a group for adults, children, or teens, watch out for the "storms" that can "sink" your group

In Chapter 5, I set out some key ideas for leading children and teen grief groups. Even leaders experienced in working with grieving adults sometimes feel overwhelmed at the thought of leading a group for children. Here you will find practical suggestions for engaging children and teens in developmentally-appropriate ways.

Chapter 6 sets out some guidelines and ideas for dealing with complicated grief in groups. In addition to summarizing the warning signs for clinical depression, you will learn ways to identify group participants who should be referred and practical suggestions for making good referrals to outside resources and professionals.

"Storms" can threaten to "sink" a grief group, so Chapter 7 develops strategies for facing four group-killers: poor marketing, ineffective group leadership skills, difficult group participants, and exhausted leaders. Because tress and burnout among leaders can derail a group, this section is crucial.

Rounding out the handbook is a resource section including reproducible handouts and an extensive annotated book list for leaders of bereavement groups.

Thank You

An effort like this never really belongs to a single author, and I would be remiss if I did not acknowledge some extraordinary people who have helped shape these ideas. First to mind, of course, are Debbie, Carolyn, and Greg—the three people who know me best and who are God's special gifts in my life. You are all patient and kind beyond measure!

The volunteers and staff of Pathways Volunteer Hospice in Long Beach, California are the people who worked alongside me in the "laboratory" where many of these ideas took shape. Your commitment to support bereaved children, teens, and adults is without equal.

For more than ten years, a group of southern California colleagues became friends and sounding board—not just for what I share here but for all of my work with bereaved people. This group led by J. William Worden has had more influence on my professional development than any other force. Thank you to Bill Worden, Barbara Smith, Stephanie Thal, Mike Meador, Linda Grant, Annette Iversen, Ann Goldman, Michelle Post, and Ron Ritter—you are indeed the "best of the best!"

One

❧ Why Grief Groups ❧

During my college days, I spent a semester working with the International Seafarers Center in the Port of Long Beach, California. I was aboard dozens of ships during those five months and met hundreds of sailors from around the world. I never tired of hearing their stories of adventure.

One story, however, stands out. The radio officer from a Danish freighter told me of the North Atlantic crossing that had most recently brought them to the United States. This trip was her last as she prepared to retire after returning to Copenhagen in the spring, having served a full career in a typically "man's world."

Though I have long sense forgotten her name, I have never forgotten her story. This trip, she reported, was the stormiest in her three-decade career on the seas. Much of their topside-stacked cargo was lost overboard as the ship pitched and rolled, tearing the cargo containers loose from their moorings.

Groups give grieving people a sense of direction in the storms of mourning

In the midst of this most harrowing experience, she seemed to have taken the storm in stride. When I inquired, she indicated that though frightened at times, she had never lost confidence: "We had accurate charts, true instruments, and an experienced crew. I never doubted we would get through the storm."

Like this Danish freighter in the North Atlantic, the experience of grief is a journey of violent "pitches and rolls." But an effective grief group and leader can give the grieving person the same sense of confidence that a seasoned sailor gets from "accurate charts, true instruments, and an experienced crew." Little by little, groups help grieving people find their "sea legs" and discover new ways to live.

When Marjorie's husband of 48 years died from pancreatic cancer, she spent several weeks, in her words, "trying to find my way." Especially during the first month after her husband's death, Marjorie's three adult children helped her with the tasks related to settling the estate. Her daughter invited Marjorie to have dinner with her own family several times each week, and one or the other of the children called nearly every day to "check on mom."

But within about six weeks, Marjorie reported, the calls came less frequently. And with the grandchildren involved in soccer and school activities, so did the invitations to dinner. When she received a call from a hospice worker, Marjorie had to admit she felt "mostly alone."

Marjorie was surprised to learn she did not have to travel the "grief journey" all by herself

"My kids want to be there for me," she told the hospice bereavement coordinator when she phoned Marjorie that day, "but they just have such busy lives. They have a lot to do besides babysitting me," she said. "They can't do this grieving for me," Marjorie said. "It's a road I'll have to walk by myself, anyway."

She was surprised, however, to find out that she didn't have to travel the road by herself. The hospice bereavement coordinator explained to Marjorie that there were at least five bereavement groups in her community—one offered by hospice, two offered by a community hospital, one at a local church, and a fifth at a nearby senior center.

Her conversation with the bereavement coordinator began a new journey for Marjorie, a journey toward healing that she learned to walk with the help of new friends in her support group. Marjorie's story is not unique, however. She is like other bereaved people, living in virtually every community.

Bereavement support groups come in all shapes and sizes. Some have been meeting weekly for many years with bereaved people constantly cycling in and out as they move along their journey in grief. Some groups focus on a particular kind of loss—such as the death of a child or the death of a loved one by suicide.

Still other groups meet for an agreed number of weeks, giving rise to their name, "time-limited groups." The facilitator in these groups leads participants through a pre-determined "agenda," covering many of the critical issues faced by people in grief.

For Reflection. . .

What do you think are the greatest values received by people who participate in a grief group?

_____

_____

_____

_____

_____

_____

_____

_____

The Value of Groups

Someone who has never participated in an effective grief support group might wonder about what benefits a group provides. "Isn't it just a bunch of sad people who sit around and cry?" they ask. Answering this criticism, here are some of the values grief groups offer to people working through bereavement.

"Normalizing" the Abnormal. Bereavement support groups help bereaved people "normalize" the experiences of grief. Through hearing others share, bereaved people realize that their experiences are not so unique and that they are not losing their mind!

Especially after their first significant loss, the recently bereaved often do not understand what "normal" is. So, if they have difficulty sleeping or find themselves not wanting to dispose of the deceased's personal possessions, the bereavement support group validates these are normal parts of bereavement.

Frequently, this normalizing does not occur by design in a group. The facilitator and veteran members realize the help they have given, only when the newer bereaved person announces, "I'm so glad I came today. Now I know I'm not going crazy since some of you have had these same feelings."

Emotional Expression. Groups provide a supportive environment for expressing emotion. Much as family members and close friends say they want to be supportive, they frequently tire of hearing the stories and often, begin advising the bereaved to "put this behind you and get on with your life. . ."

Bereavement groups provide an environment where a bereaved person can continue telling the stories and feeling sad beyond the social expectations of family and friends. The grief of bereaved parents, for example, tends to be long-lived, but well-meaning friends usually become ready to "move on" much earlier than the parents themselves. Groups provide a safe and supportive place for the emotions of grief.

Problem Solving. Groups help solve problems. One of the world's leading voices in bereavement counseling is J. William Worden. He explains that the process is really a set of "tasks," the third of which is to adjust to a life from which the deceased is missing.

Groups help people learn to live in a radically-changed world

Perhaps the longest part of the adjustment, this task requires one to learn new ways of being in the world—a world that does not include the loved person. Bereavement support groups are vital at this point because members help each other think through possible solutions to dilemmas faced by living in a changed world.

Frequently, group members exchange the names of trusted service providers for household or automobile repairs. Often, members share how they have grappled with a problem such as being expected to "get over it," or how to answer the well-intentioned advice from others like, "You'll feel better when you get pregnant again."

For Reflection. . .

What are some of the "problems" newly bereaved people face?

_____
_____
_____
_____
_____
_____
_____
_____
_____
_____
_____
_____

People Like Me. At the first meeting of a group exclusively for grieving mothers, each of the ladies in attendance remarked how she dreaded coming. One said she had felt sick to her stomach the whole day before the first meeting and almost did not come. By the end of the first meeting, however, all remarked about how these people had quickly become a caring community of friends.

What most connected these moms was the sense of shared loss. Everyone had a child die in an accident, and the support group provided a place where all understood the awful reality of that experience.

Each episode of the long-running television series, *Cheers* reminded viewers that this was a place where "everybody knows your name." Bereavement support groups function in the same way—without the corner bar! Especially in affinity groups (such as bereaved parents, widows, or suicide survivors), similar experiences provide strong support for bereavement.

Do Groups Really Help?

Some researchers have written that group participation might actually have a negative effect on people's coping with grief. In these cases, researchers have posited that possibly the constant reminders of one's loss by talking about it with others might actually be detrimental to healing. Remember, though, that this criticism is the "road not taken" syndrome—we can not know how these same individuals would have fared had they not participated in a bereavement group.

You should also be aware that this research is a minority opinion. Most documented evidence shows that groups are helpful. In her book, *Treatment of Complicated Mourning*, Therese Rando points to two studies conclusively showing the helpfulness of bereavement support services in helping people cope with the loss.

Ultimately, it is bereaved people themselves who are the best judges of whether or not groups work. The vast majority of bereaved people with whom I have interacted have said after participating for several months in a group that the group is what helped them get through it.

Groups relieve social isolation by creating a sense of "belonging." Bereavement support group participants often connect outside of the

People involved in groups usually judge the experience as pivotal in helping them work through their loss

group's official meeting times. Frequently, participants in widow groups remark within a few months that "These people are my closest friends."

Group participants often exchange phone numbers and arrange dinner or movies outside of groups, growing their friendships with each other. Even though relatively few of these become romantic relationships, the developing relationship with others in the group helps to relieve the sense of loneliness and social isolation, especially keen among the widowed bereaved.

Professional colleagues might be alarmed at this kind of interaction. Although we would always work to prevent this kind of interaction in many kinds of psychotherapy groups, grief groups operate with a different set of goals. Building new relationships and helping people create new connections are actually desired outcomes for grief groups.

Grief groups help people build new connections and new relationships

Many groups want to share phone numbers, and you are wise to let the group members manage this task themselves. If a member of the group volunteers to take on this project, encourage it and support it—but also make it clear that signing the phone list is a purely voluntary decision. Since there are significant privacy concerns in this era, do not subject your organization to potential liability by photocopying and distributing the list; let the group members do that.

Bereavement support groups work because they facilitate bereaved people supporting each other. With the guidance of a lay or professional leader, a bereavement support group becomes an important means to healing.

Two

Grief Groups: Marking the Trail

My wife loves family hikes. Whenever we visit a national park or other wilderness area, Debbie wants to make sure we make time for a short hike. We don't set out on a cross-country trek but we will often take a half-mile stroll down a well-marked trail.

I am a bit of a "city hiker." I want trails that are well-marked, level, and preferably, accompanied by a full-color trail guide. One reason I like hiking in national parks is that I can always count on getting a really nice topographical map that makes it easier to find my way.

A grief group and its leader become like a trail guide and "ranger" on this hike through grief. Especially when one is traveling in unfamiliar territory, a good trail map shows where the curves are, points out the interesting landmarks, and even warns of dangers along the way.

Those who have attended one of my workshops on grief support and counseling might remember being asked to close their eyes and point to the north. For me, the exercise is always great fun—as participants point in all different directions. When those in attendance are invited to open their eyes and look around, they usually laugh at the diversity of responses—and the "directional challenge" with which most seem to be afflicted!

Groups and their leaders become "trail guides" to people working through bereavement

In an unfamiliar room, we lack the landmarks that help us get our bearings. We become disoriented and do not know which way is which. This activity provides an excellent picture of what it means to walk the journey called grief. We are lost in unfamiliar terrain, desperately needing a compass.

Finding Direction in Grief

Whether settling frontiers or exploring new reaches of outer space, the greatest discoveries are preceded by a period in which the voyager is unsure where he is going, perhaps even a period of being completely lost. A compass is needed to find our direction in grief.

Your bereavement support group becomes a vital part of that compass. The experiences of bereavement closely parallel the directions on the compass.

The four points on a compass provide a useful picture of the grief process—remembering, reaffirming, realizing, and releasing. As the diagram shows, the grief process gradually leads to a sense of renewal. Here, the bereaved person lives with the memories, experiences the loss, and learns to live a life that no longer includes the physical presence of the loved person who has died.

Remember

Reaffirm   **Renewal**   **Realize**

Release

Remember

When we *remember* a loved one's life, we recast his or her life and the relationship shared. Recalling the significant events, the funny stories, and the occasions when survival seemed to be a long shot—all aid us in finding a place in life today for the relationship that has been disrupted by a death.

One of the most helpful resources for people in grief is their memories. Bereavement groups and other support services must provide plenty of time for people in grief to "tell their story," including the minute, mundane stories that make up a life and a relationship.

For Reflection. . .

What is your "grief story?" How do the memories of losses you have experienced make you more or less effective as a grief group leader?

_____

_____

_____

_____

_____

_____

_____

_____

Recounting these memories usually evoke some mixture of joy and sadness. We cry in telling even the funny stories and remembering the most quirky of character qualities. In early grief, both pleasant and unpleasant memories are accompanied by sadness, but it will not always be so. One goal of the grief process is being able to recall these memories without the heart-rending pain now being experienced.

Grief groups provide the opportunity for participants to share memories, stories, and photographs. Because other group members usually did not know each others' loved ones, they can hear the stories without correcting or supplementing.

Chapter Four includes questions to encourage the sharing of stories. The list includes questions like, "What are the times of day that hold the most vivid memories for you? and "When and where are you when you find yourself missing your loved one the most?"

I invite participants to bring photographs to one group meeting so we can all "meet" the people who have been important in the lives of the group members. Remembering the life of a loved one begins the process of finding direction in grief.

Reaffirm

Bereavement also calls for reaffirming of values. This compass point challenges a bereaved person to consider life's values and the spiritual "moorings" that provide an anchor in the loss. For many people, religious faith provides the cornerstone for this reaffirmation, and so they reaffirm their faith heritage through worship, prayer, or scripture reading.

Bereaved people find reaffirmation in the inspirational writings of Helen Steiner Rice, Ralph Waldo Emerson, and John Greenleaf Whittier. The melodies and lyrics of hymns and other uplifting music also provide opportunity for reflection and reaffirmation in grief. The stirring biographies of people who overcame great odds to live out their dream and purpose for life can also be very engaging for people in grief.

Whether or not a bereaved person is a "person of faith," a loved one's death evokes significant spiritual questions

The death of a loved one raises spiritual questions unlike any other of life's transitions. Even people who have given little thought to faith questions before find themselves grappling with those issues in bereavement. This exploration of faith is what provides the backdrop to reaffirmation, even when bereavement involves anger at God and cries about the seeming injustice of suffering.

While I address this matter more fully later, remember that often the road to reaffirmation includes spiritual searching or even a full-blown crisis of faith. No bereavement support group leader should be afraid to engage group participants in a discussion of how they find reaffirmation in their bereavement.

Realize

Because of our natural tendency to deny the facts of a loved one's death, the grief process also calls us to *realize* that the death has occurred. Professional grief caregivers nearly unanimously agree that seeing the body after death plays a vital role in this process of realization.

While it is helpful to see the body in a hospital bed shortly after death, my experience suggests it is also important to see the body in a casket—the most familiar symbol of death in our culture. You should be prepared for people in your group, however, for whom this experience was not possible or not chosen.

Western society is generally antagonistic to the idea of death. One poignant activity to engage in with your group is to invite them to share their favorite death euphemisms, the terms we use to avoid having to say that someone has died. Pointing out to group members that our culture is not generally very comfortable with death helps explain why so many of their friends seem at a loss for words (or at least the helpful kind!) or may even seem to avoid the grieving person altogether.

For Reflection. . .

What are some common death euphemisms people in our society use so they don't have to say "dead, died, or dies?"

_____

_____

_____

_____

_____

_____

_____

Euphemisms only serve to create confusion

Traditional symbols of mourning and the ceremonies of funerals help. The funeral procession, the service in a church or other familiar place, and the viewing of the body in a casket all aid in realizing that death has occurred and that the family and community relationships have been interrupted. Lead your group to discuss and compare the diverse funeral and memorial gatherings in which group members participated.

Saying in a group, "Funeral and memorial ceremonies help us with our grief in many different ways. Will you tell us a little today about how your family said goodbye to your loved one." Especially in a diverse group, the descriptions alone may elicit a lively discussion as group members hear about the customs practiced by other members of the group.

To follow up this discussion, I have often asked, "What parts of the ceremonies we have been talking about have worked for you? What parts of your own ceremonies did not seem to help? What parts of the other group members descriptions have you particularly liked?"

For all of their diversity, death ceremonies include some remarkably common elements in nearly all cultures. Far from being "barbaric" as some suggest, these customs provide an invaluable foundation for healing to begin.

Release

The fourth need humans share in adjusting to loss is the necessity of saying goodbye to a loved one's physical presence and the interaction possible in human relationships. In other words, we must begin to *release* our loved one as we begin to move into a world from which he or she is absent. Of course, no magical formula or "do it once, get it over with" incantation exists to say goodbye.

In some ways, we spend the rest of our lives saying goodbye

In some ways, we spend the rest of our lives saying goodbye. Going into a restaurant frequented together requires a new widower to say goodbye. Finding "new homes" for the personal possessions treasured by her son requires a bereaved mom to say goodbye. Redecorating a room filled with reminders of the relationship shared with her husband requires a young widow to say goodbye.

The process of bereavement is really about finding new, rich ways to live life fully, even in the absence of our loved ones. As J. William Worden says so well in his "tasks of mourning" approach to the grief process, we must "emotionally relocate the deceased and move on with life." This is fundamentally what "release" is all about.

Where Have the Stages Gone?

You have likely heard grief referred to as a system of "stages" through which one works, but you might have wondered about how this concept came about. Elizabeth Kübler-Ross published her groundbreaking book, *On Death and Dying* in 1969 and popularized the idea of stages, even though there has never been wide agreement about the number of stages, the names to call them, or even if such a system exists.

Even though Kübler-Ross wrote her book about the dying process rather than the grieving process, people quickly misapplied her five stages to *every* life transition. Some people used the same five stages—denial, anger, bargaining, depression, and acceptance—to explain the grief following the move to a new home, loss of a treasured possession, divorce, and job termination.

Kubler-Ross's book arrived on the scene at just the right time. Americans were engaged in a technological "space race" and the "body count" of Vietnam was a regular feature of the nightly news. Americans wanted simple, easy categories to label experiences that defy labeling. The technological advances of the 50's and 60's begged for easy categories and Kübler-Ross' stages provided an easy way to characterize the grief process.

By the mid-1970's, however, people working in clinical settings and writing about grief counseling realized the pitfalls of categorizing grief in terms of "stages." While the system suggested an easy way to refer to people, the process of adjusting life to a significant loss was simply too complex to reduce to easy boxes.

If the "stages" were made broad enough that a few of them described the whole process, they were so general as to not provide any real direction for counselors. If the stages were specific enough to provide direction, they were so narrow that there would be many of them and some people would undoubtedly skip over several, making the model virtually useless for caregivers.

In addition, a "stage" describes a passive process—something I am "in" rather than something I can work through. Unfortunately, passive language intensifies the feeling that a bereaved person is a victim of his or her circumstances. While no one would choose to have a loved one die, bereaved people must realize that their *response* to the loss is very much within their control. Creating a climate where people can make these positive choices is one of the things grief groups do best.

Because bereavement is about people and relationships, easy categories and stages usually do not fit

For Reflection. . .

What are some of the misconceptions you had about grief before you experienced your first significant loss? Do you think these are typical?

_____

_____

_____

_____

_____

_____

_____

Many of your group members will arrive at a group session confused about "stages of grief." Perhaps they have read a book or article or someone has explained to him or her, "Well you're in the 'anger stage' right now. . ." One of the greatest gifts we give is to clarify that there is no broad agreement about how to label these stages or even if such a concept exists.

Grief is a collision of every possible emotion

Professional and volunteer counselors are constantly grappling with ways to describe the process of adjustment that places the responsibility for growth squarely on the shoulders of the bereaved. Even recent research attempts at defining a predictable process have raised as many questions as answers. In the end, we must conclude that the grieving person is really the only true expert on grief—at least his or her own.

Grief –Emotions and a Whole Lot More

If you interview 100 people on the street and ask them to define grief, 95 of them will describe the experience in emotional terms. Sadness, loss, sorrow, and depression will be the words most chosen. Indeed, grief is about emotion.

In fact, grief is really a collision of every emotion. Sadness, loneliness, love, fear, uncertainty, abandonment, anger, guilt, and peacefulness are just a few of the emotions experienced by people in grief.

As you work with grieving people, you will notice a few emotions that are common to the experience. Far from being stages of grief, these emotions are interwoven throughout the bereavement process for most people.

Perhaps most obvious in grief is *sadness*. Regardless of how long a person was ill or how great a relief death is for overwhelmed caregivers, bereaved people feel sadness at the death of a loved one. The words *bereaved* and *bereft* originate in terms that mean *to be robbed*—and that is exactly the feeling of grief.

This sadness or yearning originates both from missing the deceased person and from contemplating a future without him or her. In early grief, a bereaved person has not experienced enough life without the deceased to know what it will be like, so this sadness or yearning is mostly about what she imagines life will be like without his physical presence in her life. As days and weeks pass, the sadness intensifies as the reality of his death confirms the experience of loss she imagined.

In leading groups, keep in mind that not every relationship is treasured. Sometimes, sadness is not as much about what a bereaved person lost as it is about what he never had. When abuse or substance addiction characterized the relationship, the faint hope that one day "things would be different" is shattered by the finality of death.

Remember that not every relationship is a treasured one, so some of what is lost is that which was never possessed

Anger is also common among grieving people. The anger may be directed at healthcare professionals, friends or family members, or God. Though difficult for most grieving people to admit, they may experience intense anger at their loved one for dying. This anger may be even more pronounced if the deceased loved one's actions hastened death such as in a suicide or when the deceased was careless about health matters.

In some communities and families, anger is seen as so negative that it is sent underground rather than being expressed. Your group might be the place where grieving people have the freedom to say what is really in their heart—even when those words are not acceptable among the people with whom the grieving person lives.

Guilt can also be particularly strong during grief, invading when the bereaved person thinks she should have done or said something different. You have undoubtedly heard these expressions that indicate the grieving person is grappling with guilt:

- "If I had insisted she go to the doctor earlier, they could have done something."

- "If only I had been home, I could have called the paramedics."

- "That's the car I gave him for graduation—and now that's the car that cost him his life."

Part of supporting people in grief is realizing that some guilt makes sense. While it is never appropriate to judge the reasonableness of another person's guilt feelings, it is possible that the there is a good reason for some guilt. Most of these regrets and guilt feelings subside in weeks or months—especially as the bereaved begins to see the death in the context of an entire lifetime of relationship.

A skilled counselor may encourage the grieving person to seek forgiveness from the deceased by writing a letter of apology. Recalling memories from the life shared also helps with guilt feelings. If these feelings of guilt seem to persist in spite of group involvement, a referral to a skilled counselor with expertise in grief and loss is in order.

Fear often breaks through in bereavement. A bereaved person may be scared of the future, changes in relationships, and new responsibilities now carried. One of the benefits of a grief group is that these common fears are normalized in the discussion with other grieving people. In addition, because grief groups have an ability to "problem-solve," group participants can learn simple strategies for making sure locks are in good working order and that the home is secure.

When discussing fears about illness, you will want to point out the importance of a thorough physical examination a few months after a loved one's death. This will rule out physical illness and help to alleviate fears about getting sick, perhaps with the same illness that took the loved one's life, which is also a common fear for grieving people.

Loneliness is perhaps the most persistent of the emotions of grief, tending to catch the bereaved person when she least expects it. The sense of being "on my own" is palpable, especially at significant times of year like holidays and anniversaries. Hearing a favorite song or smelling the aroma of a familiar food becomes the means by which the bereaved recall pleasant memories of life with the loved one.

Group members are probably grappling with sadness, anger, guilt, fear, loneliness—and a whole lot more

These emotions and several dozen others are often experienced as part of the grief process. Remember that every person experiences grief somewhat uniquely, and there are no timetables or chronological stages through which one must "progress." Part of your job as a bereavement support group leader is to remind group participants that grief is the normal and natural response to a major loss in life.

Grief is far more than emotion, however. The process of readjusting life after a significant loss is holistic, engaging every part of our being—physical, spiritual, relational, mental, and emotional.

For Reflection. . .

In addition to the emotional components of grief described here, what are some other emotions you have observed in yourself or some other person who is dealing with a significant loss?

_____
_____
_____
_____
_____
_____
_____
_____

Bereavement engages every part of the person—emotional, social, spiritual, physical, and cognitive

Grief and Physical Well-Being

Grief is experienced physically in a variety of ways. Tears, knots in the stomach, tightness in the throat or chest, and intense fatigue are a few of the ways people experience grief physically. Group members need to be encouraged that these physical sensations are a normal part of grief. However, if a group member is worried about a symptom, always encourage him to see his doctor for a thorough check-up.

Grief group participants describe a diversity of experiences with sleep. Often, insomnia becomes a "vicious circle" when the bereaved person, having difficulty sleeping, begins worrying about not sleeping. The worry, then, makes it even more difficult to fall asleep and the cycle intensifies.

Of course, sleep disruption can be a symptom of an anxiety disorder or clinical depression. Most bereavement-related insomnia, however, is a temporary condition brought about by the intense mental processing of this overwhelming experience. Insomnia is sometimes magnified for those who work at distracting themselves from the grief all day, only to fall in bed at night and then start thinking about everything that has been put aside throughout the day.

Helpful questions to ask grief group members are,

- ◆ "What are the changes you've most noticed in your eating, sleeping, and exercising habits since your loved one died?"

- ◆ "How are you managing the physical challenges of grief like sleeplessness, fatigue, and loss of appetite?"

How Grief Changes Relationships

No matter how strong friendships were before a loved one's death, some friends will surely disappoint in the early months of bereavement. Relationships change for many different reasons.

Bereaved parents report feeling abandoned by parents who have children the same age as the one who died. Perhaps these parents feel some strange sense of guilt that "our child is still alive" (called survivor guilt). Perhaps being around a bereaved parent causes a friend to realize that a child's life comes with no guarantees and that the same experience could befall any parent.

For many reasons, the bereaved person's best friends might be strangely silent in this loss

Perhaps friends feel vulnerable to the same emotion and tears that so often seize a bereaved person. Friends of the bereaved often are afraid to talk about the deceased for fear their own sadness will further depress the bereaved.

Group members will frequently complain about friends who want them to go to dinner every night, almost as if the newly-bereaved person is helpless. On the other extreme, group members will report that some friends ignore them altogether. Whatever the reason, disappointment alters relationships.

One issue to address in support groups is how to relate to friends who disappoint. Remind group members that most insensitive remarks come from people trying to show that they care. Even bereaved people have to learn to look past the *behavior* to see the *intent*. People generally say and do insensitive things—not because they do not *care* but because they do not *know*.

"I Must Be Going Crazy:" Grief and the Mind

Lack of concentration, memory lapses, and inability to make good decisions are just a few of the ways bereaved people feel challenged mentally. You will notice people in your group will often express the fear, "I think I'm losing my mind," and then cite forgetfulness or loss of focus as "proof" of their "breakdown."

Grief group members help each other by normalizing this concern. As the group leader, you can reinforce the discussion by explaining that stress often causes these symptoms and that the death of a loved one is among life's most stressful events. Forgetfulness and lack of concentration are common themes among the bereaved.

During group meetings, encourage participants to talk about how their mental state has been altered by bereavement with questions like,

- "What are the things you are having the most trouble remembering?"

- "How are you dealing with the typical lack of concentration in grief?"

Remind grieving people that forgetfulness and loss of concentration are common difficulties

"Where Is God Now?" Spiritual Challenges in Grief

Bereavement involves spiritual reaffirmation, but frequently on the way to rediscovering spiritual purpose comes a great test of belief. Especially when the death was seen as untimely or particularly "unfair," the bereaved person likely grapples with significant spiritual issues.

During my work as a pastor, I did not appreciate this "spiritual seeking" common in grief. About six and a half years into my pastoral ministry, Debbie and I experienced two late miscarriages about 15 months apart. The first was difficult; the second was devastating.

Both of us engaged in ministry and possessing advanced theological degrees, one would have thought we would be able to live through that experience and simply express the confidence of some, "God is in control and I will trust Him in this experience." That was not the case.

Because our first baby had died, friends and colleagues in ministry all over the United States were praying for us during the second pregnancy. If ever a family had been "covered" in prayer, ours was. I think that was part of the devastation of the second loss; in spite of people pleading with the Lord for the safety of this child, God still said, "No." That was beyond my comprehension.

In fact, God and I had quite a discussion about that issue (actually, it was more a diatribe on my part than a discussion!) In my railing at God, I said something like, "Your employee benefit program stinks! I can do better than this—and not have to put up with all the stuff of ministry—if I work at Boeing!"

But somewhere along the way in the weeks and months that followed, when Debbie and I could not really feel the warm presence of the Lord we served, He ministered to us in very loving ways. God's concern for us was expressed through the lives of a few friends who made meals and held our hands and cried with us. When we couldn't feel His touch, He touched us through those people.

Bereaved people are comforted deeply in realizing people come because they care rather than because they are just paid to provide care

One reason I am so committed to the equipping of bereavement volunteers in churches is because Debbie and I have experienced first-hand what a valuable ministry it is for people to go to the "brokenhearted," not because they are *paid* to be there but because they *want* to be there.

Meaning-making is the term used most often to refer to the spiritual searching that is part of the grief process. Sometimes this search lasts for months or even years. Often, I have found, this search for meaning eventually involves seeking or granting forgiveness in relationships with the deceased, other people, or even from God.

In grief groups, leaders of religious and secular grief groups alike can engage participants in talking about what their spiritual struggles have been. Some of my favorite questions are,

- "What has been the biggest spiritual struggle of the grief journey for you so far?"

◆ "In what ways do you think your personal faith/belief system has been strengthened or challenged in your grief?"

Some group members say they have not had significant spiritual struggles in their grief. Keep in mind that such a person might be tempted to "scold" others for expressing their doubts and struggles.

For Reflection. . .

Which of the components of the bereavement experience—emotional, physical, social, mental, or spiritual have you found most difficult in your own experiences with loss?

_____

_____

_____

_____

_____

_____

_____

People experience grief in very unique ways. For some, the biggest challenges are in their highly unpredictable emotional states while others struggle with eating or sleeping habits. Some grieving people are most distressed by their spiritual struggles or with the response of their friends. Leaders of grief groups sponsored by faith communities will want to be sensitive to and acknowledge the possibility of these struggles, especially when suggesting the group pray together. Many inner struggles and concerns are never verbalized.

The grief group's role—and your role as a group leader—is not to "fix" grieving people. The role is to provide a safe haven, a place where grieving people can feel free to express whatever they are experiencing without fear of judgment and unkind correction.

My Reflections. . .

Pausing to reflect helps nourish the spirit and provide vision for the future

Three

➷ Establishing Groups ↳

When John was hired as the first—and only—social worker for a new hospice program, the administrator explained her hope that he would get a grief group started right away. The administrator believed a community bereavement support group would not only help the families served by Hospice of the Valley, but that the group would also help the agency become better known in the community.

John was an experienced medical social worker who had worked with individuals for most of his six years in a hospital setting. He had even led a few support groups when he was interning in graduate school. But bereavement groups were a whole new arena for him—and he hardly knew where to begin.

Whether professional or volunteer, you might share some of John's anxiety. His questions might be similar to your own, so I have chosen here to work through some of the most important issues to consider in beginning a bereavement support group.

"Aim at nothing—and you'll be sure to hit it every time!"

Identify the Group's Purposes

In the late 1980's, organizations of every size and type invested extensive staff time in drafting lengthy, detailed "mission statements." I remember waiting long enough at one fast food restaurant to read their entire mission statement, undoubtedly painstakingly drafted in an executive retreat, reproduced in 10-point type, and framed above the counter.

While I waited, I was especially drawn to the paragraph about "fast, courteous service where every customer is treated as our special guest." Whenever I have visited this chain, I have experienced none of the fast, courteous service and have been treated like anything other than an honored guest! Sometimes the gulf is wide between vision and implementation!

What I applaud in this effort, however, is that the organization's leadership clearly articulated what they wanted their people to accomplish. A mentor of mine was fond of saying, "If you aim at nothing, you'll hit it every time!"

One gift of a group to bereaved people is the feeling that they are not alone in their grief

For Reflection. . .

Write down your most important reasons for starting a grief group. What are you hoping to see happen in people's lives? What will you get out of leading this group?

_____
_____
_____
_____
_____
_____
_____

Reflecting on the following purposes may help you refine and articulate what you want your group to accomplish. Your objectives become the standard for evaluating the group's success.

- **Provide emotional support to the bereaved.** The best bereavement support groups create a climate of safety where participants feel free to express the range of experiences in grief. A group best provides emotional support when group members can consistently leave a group gathering feeling that they are not alone and that there has been freedom to express emotions and thoughts that some see as negative.

- **Educate grieving people about the process.** Since everyone's grief is unique, you will want your group to affirm the personal nature of grief. Effective groups educate participants about common components of grief. As group members share their experiences, the participants learn that, in grief, there is wide latitude in the term "normal."

♦ **Encourage social interaction**. A vital part of the grief process is about saying goodbye to relationships that have now changed. Grief is also about developing new friendships and finding a common bond with people who understand and care. Effective groups encourage these relationships to develop outside the group time, and often plan activities and events—movies, dinners out, and day trips for example—to foster the development of this community.

♦ **Develop positive problem-solving skills**. In his book by the same title, Thomas Attig writes that grief is about "relearning the world." Group members learn new problem-solving skills through support groups. Because the support group becomes a community of mutual help, participants share ideas about such practical matters as home and auto maintenance, estate taxes, and where to secure good business advice.

In groups I lead, I watch the boundary between a participant saying on the one hand, "This is what worked for me" and on the other hand, "This is what you ought to do." Remind participants that sharing ideas is helpful but advice-giving is not.

Sharing ideas is helpful; giving advice is not

Should Our Group Go On Forever?

New group leaders must answer the question, "How long should this group meet?" At the beginning, leaders need to decide whether a group will be an ongoing, open-ended group or a time-limited group with a specific ending date. Then, group leaders will want to communicate that structure to potential participants when describing the group.

Ongoing or open-ended groups are very effective with bereaved people. These groups meet indefinitely, and generally encourage people to come as often as they want, for as long as they want. Twelve-step groups like Alcoholics Anonymous and nationally-affiliated bereavement groups like The Compassionate Friends are ongoing groups. Here are a few of the features of this group structure to consider:

- Since people come and go, there is less pressure to be present every time the group meets. However, remember this "come-when-you-want" attitude can work against building a supportive community, since people need consistent time together to develop trust and feel supported.

- Because grief veterans—those who have been attending the group for several months—are mixed in with people who are newer to the grief process, modeling occurs. One participant in a senior widows and widowers group said he got great fulfillment out of being a "symbol" to newer widows and widowers that they would survive, even after becoming widowed in the sixtieth year of marriage.

- Ongoing groups allow people to join at any time so a person who feels ready to join a group does not have to wait weeks or months for the next group cycle.

- Group leaders can naturally use the calendar to address important themes. The group can discuss coping skills for the approaching holidays in the late fall. In the spring as bereaved people are thinking about Mothers Day and Fathers Day, group leaders can again address holiday tips. In open-ended groups, though group membership tends to be fluid, necessitating a readdressing of key concepts throughout the year. Listen for clues about what the current participants need from the group.

Holidays like Mothers Day, Fathers Day, Christmas, and Valentine's Day yield important discussions for grief groups

The other type of group format is a *time-limited group*, a bereavement support group that meets for a pre-determined number of sessions spaced at perhaps weekly or bi-weekly intervals. Here are some of the features that contribute to and detract from this group structure's effectiveness:

- Grieving people who are reticent to join a support group will more likely join a group where there is a definite ending date. Some people are afraid to join a group because they think they are signing on for life! Many are attracted to the notion of a known ending point.

- Group leaders can be very intentional about covering important topics in time-limited groups. With some planning, a group leader can be certain that the group talks about physical challenges in grief, unique challenges of holiday grief, the importance of building new relationships, and ways to handle anger or guilt. In a time-limited group, a leader asks participants at the first group meeting what they consider to be the most important issues to discuss, and then tailors the group meetings to address those expressed needs.

- Since group members make a commitment to attend all sessions, people can build effective supportive communities fairly quickly. I observed two bereaved moms whose teenage children had died in crashes become one another's best support after only a couple of meetings. For months after the group officially concluded, these two ladies had lunch together, called or visited each other on holidays, and acknowledged the anniversaries of the other child's death.

When choosing a time-limited format, do not allow the group to add on a few more meetings. Invariably, some group participants will say they wish the group did not end so soon, proof that the group has become a community of support.

Bereavement isn't magically finished in a year—or any other social time frame!

Encourage ongoing conversation and the exchanging of phone numbers but do not agree to lengthen the group. Start a new group if needed after a break of a few weeks, but keep your word to end when you said the group would end so people do not feel trapped.

When Should Group Members Move On?

One common issue faced by leaders is how to help group members move on when the group itself might be impeding the grief process. I believe there are several distinct issues here.

The grief process is far too personal to suggest that participants should quit attending the group, say by the first anniversary of their loved one's death. I was shown a form letter sent by the bereavement coordinator of a large urban hospice program to a man whose wife had died a year earlier.

In short, the letter said since it had now been a year, he should get out of the group to make room for newer people. I was aghast at this "standard of care," but since several members of that group began attending a group I led after receiving the same letter, I concluded it must be a "company policy."

For Reflection. . .

When are some times you would consider telling a group participant that they should stop attending? Why would you "draw a line" at that point?"

_____

_____

_____

_____

_____

_____

_____

If your group becomes a community of friends, expect these friends to want to be together

By the end of six months or a year, some bereaved people are just becoming ready to participate in a support group. To suggest group participants should be within the first year or two since the death is to enforce a standard that cannot be justified.

Keep in mind that some bereaved people will continue to attend the group because it has become an important social outlet for them. The group has become a community of friends and the loyalty can run deep since these were the people "who were there for me when I most needed it." Encouraging interaction like group dinners and day-trips can help participants continue the social interaction they crave.

Remember also that some group members keep coming because they do not know how to stop! Inertia and habit are powerful forces. When I detect a group member might be attending out of habit more than need, I try to ask the person privately, "You have been coming for a while now. Is our group still helping you? How?"

I also try to assure group members they can come as long as they feel they are learning and growing. But with this assurance, I try to explain to the group regularly, "There will come a time when you will not need this group. When that day comes, it is okay to say

◆ 32 ◆

goodbye to us." I am amazed that every time I have said something like that to the group, one or two members approach me in the next week or two to say that is how they have been feeling.

When a long-time group member decides he no longer needs the group, I ask him to come one more time to say goodbye to the group. He needs to express gratitude to the group and they need to know that he feels he is now ready to "graduate," not that he is leaving because of hurt feelings.

In the ongoing groups that I have led, one technique I have used is to take a four-week hiatus, usually during the summer. I discovered the benefit of this several years ago when I was teaching an intensive summer course for a local college and knew I would be unable to be at my afternoon group for about five weeks.

For a month before the date my college course was to begin, I told the group of my inability to meet with them for those weeks and even offered to get another facilitator to lead the group. Several participants were planning to be away part of that month, and others indicated a break would be helpful. I provided a list of other nearby groups that would be meeting during the month of August for those who wanted to try a different group.

The last meeting before our break, we held a "party" because we knew a few of our group members would not be coming back when the group resumed a few weeks later. This gave each of us an opportunity to say goodbye to each other as we shared some of what the group had meant to us—whether attending a few weeks or many months. About two-thirds of the group members returned when the group resumed in the fall, while the others gracefully "bowed out."

Build in opportunities for group members to say goodbye so they can leave the group when they are ready to leave

Throughout the years, I have led bereavement groups following both closed-ended and ongoing formats. Each has its benefits and liabilities, but ultimately, both formats work well to support people in grief.

In beginning a bereavement support group of either type, you will want to consider some logistical concerns. Here are a few items to be certain not to overlook. . .

Groups of six to ten. Effective support groups offer adequate time for people to tell their own story and to get to know one another. Groups of two or three have a difficult time normalizing the range of grief experiences because there simply are not enough people to offer much diversity. On the other hand, groups that exceed ten or eleven participants rarely have time in a group meeting for everyone to speak. I have found the optimum size for a bereavement support group is between six and ten regular participants.

Warm, neutral locations. Grief support groups function well in a wide variety of environments because ultimately, the support comes from the people, not from the room. That being said, however, keep in mind that an auditorium with 500 seats will create a big obstacle to the intimacy and warmth you want to foster.

Community centers and churches often have small conference rooms that are ideal for a bereavement support group. Some banks and libraries also have community rooms that work well. A well-known facility on a well-traveled route is best.

Consider the furnishings in the room, as well. A conference table can give people a "prop" so they do not feel quite so vulnerable. Tables also create spaces for activities like sharing photos, writing in a journal, or creating art. Comfortable chairs and couches create a warm, "family room" environment that helps people relax.

No location is ideal for everyone but the room doesn't make the group

Remember that no location is ideal for everyone. Younger people might resist attending a group at a senior center while people from a different belief system might be apprehensive about attending a group at a church. Grieving people are usually highly motivated to seek help, so the location will not usually impede those who are open to group participation.

Light refreshments. Food and drinks have value in helping people connect with others. Most families and many clubs eat when they gather.

For Reflection. . .

Now that you have considered group size and location, where are you thinking of holding your group? How many people would you expect to be involved?

_____

_____

_____

_____

_____

_____

_____

At the first meeting, you might consider having coffee and a light snack like cookies, pretzels, or snack crackers. If participants seem to enjoy the snack, invite them to take turns bringing a snack to share.

No longer than 90 minutes. Decide in advance how long each meeting will last and stick to that time parameter. Support group meetings should probably not exceed 90 minutes. People can become easily overwhelmed by over-long meetings, so make sure you practice active leadership and keep the meetings "on track."

Do not allow meetings to run past the established ending time, no matter how well the conversation is going. People lead busy lives and are embarrassed by having to leave before a meeting ends. If you say the meeting will end at 8:30, do not keep people until 8:40.

Costs. Whether or not to charge for group participation can be a particularly thorny issue. Even non-profit organizations, the most frequent sponsors of groups, do not always agree. Some believe that charging is a violation of their community purpose and perhaps their tax status. Other organizations see a low "materials" fee as a way to help group members underwrite a small part of the costs and perceive greater value in the service.

Meetings that go on too long wear out both the participants and the leadership

Therapists usually charge for group participation in accordance with their regular professional fees—their hourly rate divided by the anticipated attendance, for example.

Whatever you decide to charge, communicate openly and fairly about the fees, and consider in advance how to handle those who indicate financial hardship.

For Reflection. . .

What do you think about fees for participating in a grief group? Which of your values do you think are most reinforced or most violated by charging for people to participate?

_____

_____

_____

_____

_____

_____

_____

_____

_____

_____

Determining Who Should Come: Screening Participants

One vital issue that arises in leading a group is determining who "fits" with the group (and with the facilitator's skill level) and who would be better served by other community resources. Here are some questions to ask in prescreening participants:

Don't be afraid to screen participants. No group is right for everybody

- *How long has it been since the loss?* People who are less than four to six weeks post-death often have difficulty participating in a grief support group, but there is no hard-and-fast rule. You might try encouraging people to wait a few weeks but let them make the final decision on when they are ready.

- *How did you find out about our group?* The answer to this question may give insight into what other "help" the bereaved person is getting. This question also assists in evaluating the effectiveness of your marketing efforts.

- *What are you hoping the group will help you with?* Does the bereaved person's purpose for a group match your group's purpose? Keep in mind, however, that bereaved people often don't know what to expect—in grief or from a group, so don't lean too heavily on their responses.

- *Is a therapist or other counselor helping you with your grief?* This will often be the person who referred the grieving person to the group, and he/she may feel group interaction will be a helpful adjunct to therapy. You might also ask if the bereaved has worked with a counselor or therapist before since this might provide clues about the individual's mental health history.

- *What did you and your therapist conclude about what you needed then?* If the potential group member has seen a mental health professional, this question is kinder than the direct, "So what was your problem?!" Clinical professionals should be wary of including group members with long-term mental health diagnoses. Volunteer group leaders should always seek the advice of their supervisor before including in the group a person with a long-term mental health diagnosis.

My Reflections. . .

Pausing to reflect helps nourish the spirit and provide vision for the future

Four

What Do You Do in a Grief Group?

Leadership of a bereavement support group depends on your personality and skills. Ultimately, you and the group participants are far better served when you take stock of your own style and lead the group accordingly, rather than trying to imitate some other person, regardless of how much you respect him or her.

People coming to a bereavement group generally seem to want an active leader. They do not need someone to tell them what to do, but they do desire a leader who will take charge and lead. Passivity on the part of the leader will probably only increase the anxiety level of new group members and allow a "Monopolizing Mary" to wrest leadership of the group from the appointed facilitator.

One agenda that works well is this:

* At the official starting time (not one minute past), welcome the participants and introduce yourself. Include a notation about who sponsors the group.

* Invite all participants to tell their name (first name is fine) and say a word or two about the loss that brought them to the group. If you choose, at the first meeting you may also want to ask each participant to share *one* hope they have for the group. In closed-ended groups where you don't have new participants joining after the second or third meeting, you may not need to repeat the

Lead the group in line with your skills and personality instead of imitating someone else name-sharing at every meeting since people will know each other's names.

- ◆ Briefly describe the topic of the day and how you'll be "getting into it" (key question, reading a story/quotation, brief presentation, etc.) For example, you might say, "Today we're going to start out our discussion by talking about feeling crazy in grief."

- ◆ At the group's first meeting, share your expectation of "ground rules" and ask group members to add to the list. At subsequent meetings, remind group members of the key rules, especially if you've been having trouble at earlier meetings with one or more of the rules. (See below for some possible ground rules).

Asking key questions is almost always the best way to keep a group meeting on track

- ◆ Ask your key question, perhaps prefaced by two or three statements. For example, you might say, "Many people in grief say they feel they have lost their mind. We can't remember where anything is, drive around aimlessly forgetting where we are going, and have difficulty concentrating. What about your grief so far has made you feel like you are losing your mind?"

- ◆ About two-thirds through the group time, I will often say something like, "We've not heard from a couple of you today. Now might be a good time if you have something you want to say. . ." As you get to know your group members, you will probably recognize some people have great richness in what they say but need encouragement to talk. I often will say, "Dave, a penny for your thoughts. . ." or similar "drawing-out" words (Chapter 7 includes ideas for engaging "quiet" participants).

- ◆ Ten minutes before the published ending time, begin drawing the meeting to a close. Some people close the meeting with a reading, a brief summary of the topic, or everyone joining hands and reciting the Serenity Prayer. Whatever you do, however, *end on time or ahead of time every time!*

Group Ground Rules

Making sure group participants have a clear understanding of group rules can save you a great deal of grief in your leadership role. In his book, *Grief Counseling and Grief Therapy*, J. William Worden refers to these group agreements as the ground rules for the group.

Here are a few rules to consider. Ask your group members to add to the list and request their help in enforcing the rules.

1. Attend all meetings and arrive on time (some open-ended groups adopt a "drop in" format allowing people to come whenever they want; if this is your format, simply adapt this rule accordingly)

2. Share as much or as little about your loss experience as you want; no one has to talk

3. Advice should be given only after gaining permission (i.e. "Do you want to hear what some of the group members have done about that?")

4. What is said in the group, stays in the group

5. Talk about your own stories and experiences and limit what you say about people not in our group. You are the one coming to the group and you will get the most help if you talk about your experiences.

6. Socialize outside the group as much as you want—but remember Rule # 4!

7. Do not apply your meanings and beliefs to other people's stories. Let them assign the meaning they are ready to assign at that point. In other words, don't say, "Well at least he isn't suffering any more" or similar statements.

8. Like in kindergarten (where we learned everything we need for life!) only one person speaks at a time

Group rules create a sense that the group is an emotionally safe arena for talking about the experiences of grief

The eighth rule seems to be the hardest to enforce as group members are sometimes prone to start side-conversations while others are talking. There is no substitute for gently—but firmly—confronting this when it occurs. If not, your group will quickly dissolve into chaos. The section on difficult people in Chapter Seven will provide more practical help.

Topics and Questions

I like starting group meetings with a key question, usually with some introductory remarks about why I have chosen it. A key question is often all that is needed to start a rich discussion. These can be used at the beginning of the group after participants have introduced themselves or when the discussion "stalls" during the meeting time.

Even when the group wanders far away from the chosen topic, respect the needs expressed by group members

Sometimes, the discussion will wander far afield of these questions. A facilitator must always remain alert to the participants' needs and decide whether or not to "bring the discussion back" to the topic. As a rule of thumb, I try once during the time to "return home," but if the conversation reverts to the other topic, that is where we stay.

Always remember that the group belongs to the participants, and not to you as a leader. They are the ones who stand to gain the most by participation, and they likely know what the issues are with which they struggle most. Trust them.

Frequently, I set up the question with two or three sentences about why the topic is important. For instance, after everyone has introduced themselves and offered a brief introduction about their loss, I might say:

> Many people find anger to be one of the most troubling emotions in grief. Some of us were taught as children that anger is okay, while others of us learned that it is inappropriate. Yet, anger is a gigantic piece of the bereavement puzzle for many people. What and when do you find yourself feeling the most anger and how do you find yourself expressing it?

Asking poignant, open-ended questions is one of the most important skills that must be developed among counselors and support group leaders. Engaging questions invite the grieving person to tell her story. Questions that cannot be easily answered with one or two words make it possible for leaders to do less talking and more listening.

The best remedy to lots of silence and "dead time" in groups is for the leader to always be ready with two or three key questions. Even though asking a question like, "How was your week?" is an open-ended question that begs more than a yes or no answer, the question is vague, making it hard for grieving people to respond. In the examples below, you will notice that most of the questions ask for specific details and encourage the person in grief to tell his or her story. They can be asked both as "meeting openers" and as discussion questions when the conversation stalls.

The best questions ask for specific details and invite the telling of the bereaved person's story

- ◆ Where and when did you meet? Did someone introduce you or did you just find each other?

- ◆ What were your favorite holidays? What did you do together? Which special days do you expect to be/are you finding to be the hardest in your grief?

- ◆ Where were your favorite places to go? What did you most enjoy about those places?

- ◆ What was the best gift ever given to you by this person? What was the best gift you ever gave him/her?

- ◆ What did you find most meaningful/least meaningful about the funeral? Where was it held? What would you do differently?

- How do you find yourself dealing with anger in your grief and when do you find it causes you the most trouble?

- What has been the biggest adjustment for you so far?

- What are the two or three fondest memories you have of your loved one?

- What scares you the most about this experience?

- In what ways do you hope you have left a heritage for your children/community/etc.? In what ways did your loved one leave their mark on the world?

- If grief were no longer an issue for you, what do you think would be most different in your life?

- Who has been most supportive to you so far? What have they done to show that support?

- In what ways do you wish your friends or family members would act differently toward you right now?

- What has been the most challenging to you in your faith/belief system (your faith, your philosophy, your perspective on God, etc.?) How do you think your beliefs have been strengthened by this?

- What is the dumbest thing anyone has said to you and how would you now respond to the same comment?

- What are the loneliest times for you and what are you doing with them?

- What is the part of life with your loved one you are now missing most?

- How is it for you when someone says something like, "His/her death must be a relief for you?" Are there ways that is true for you? How?

- What are you doing about your loved one's personal things like clothes, jewelry, and toiletries? Have you started the process of finding new homes for those things or deciding what to keep and what to discard?

- Of all the personal items that belonged to him/her, what is the most special item for you? What do you not have that you wish you did?

Inviting grieving people to tell their stories is one of the important gifts groups offer

♦ Where in your grief do you most often confront guilt and regrets? What have you found most helpful to get through those times?

♦ How would people around you know you are sad? Is that a true picture of the "real you?"

♦ What expectations do you have of yourself in your grief? Are you thinking your expectations for life are realistic right now? Why or why not?

♦ What are the changes you've most noticed in your eating, sleeping, and exercising habits since your loved one died? How are you managing the physical challenges of grief like sleeplessness, fatigue, and loss of appetite?

What follows are eight "Group Ideas." These suggestions are intended to give you a roadmap on how to get started with your group. There are few absolutes here; create activities and discussion points that fit the personality of your group, your passions, and your skill level.

Group Idea 1: First Meeting

Like all of the bereavement group meetings, you'll want to begin this group with an opportunity for people to get to know each other and each others' stories. The following will give you an idea of how to begin the group in an effective way.

There are a couple of important considerations for you as the group leader.

Arrive early. Nothing produces anxiety for new group participants like not knowing who is in charge

   ♦ Arrive early (at least 15 minutes) and welcome people as they come
   ♦ Begin on time and end on time (don't punish on-timers by waiting for late-comers)
   ♦ Encourage people to tell their own stories and discourage discussion of the experiences of people who are not in the group
   ♦ Remind people often of the need for keeping confidences
   ♦ Encourage everyone to share but force no one

At the time for the group to begin, welcome people and introduce yourself. Gather people into a circle or around a table. Introduce yourself and tell briefly either 1) about the most recent loss you have had, or 2) why you feel "called" to work with bereaved people. Then, ask folks to go around the circle with this statement: "Please tell us your name and a word or two about the loss that brought you to our group."

At any meeting where there are new people—and that certainly includes the first meeting of a new group—I briefly explain the format. An explanation reduces the participants' anxiety about not knowing what to expect next.

> "We'll begin by introducing ourselves and reacquainting ourselves with each other's stories, much like we've done tonight. Then, I'll offer a brief explanation of what we're going to talk about tonight, ask a key question to help us focus our discussion, and then provide some summary ideas at the end."

> "Tonight, I would like to ask you to consider and then briefly share about this question: What do you find so far has been the most difficult part of grief or the part of grief that most troubles you."

Summarize—from what you have experienced, what you have learned, and what the group members have shared

During the meeting, encourage people to join in. Ask follow-up questions and clarifying questions like:

- How does Mary's experience compare with the rest of you?

- Could you tell us a bit more about what you mean by that?

- Do we understand you to say. . .?

- In what ways do you sense that getting better or worse as you continue your grief journey?

Summarize the meeting with some of the ideas you have learned or read earlier in this handbook about the nature of grief. If people have already discussed these at length, you might just want to summarize these now.

- Grief is not well understood in our society

- Grief includes all of life: emotional, physical, social, mental, and spiritual

◆ Resolving grief is a long-term process. We do not really ever "recover from" or "get over" our losses, but we do learn to live in this new set of circumstances. Life can be good again, but after a significant loss, we must learn to live in a new world that does not include the person who died.

Group Idea 2: Dealing With Anger in Grief

Like all of the bereavement group meetings, you'll want to begin this group with an opportunity for people to get to know each other and each others' stories. Remember to arrive early, begin on time, and end on time.

Explain the group's format with words like, "We'll begin by introducing ourselves and reacquainting ourselves with each other's stories. Then, I'll offer a brief explanation of what we're going to talk about tonight, ask a key question to help us focus our discussion, and then provide some summary ideas at the end."

"Tonight, I would like to ask you to consider and then briefly share about this question: How do you find yourself dealing with anger in your grief and when do you find it causes you the most trouble?"

You can listen for themes and suggestions. Then, briefly summarize what participants have been discussing.

Help group members understand the normal physical experiences of grief like sleep difficulties and loss of appetite

Group Idea 3: Grief and Physical Well-Being

After giving group participants an opportunity to tell their name and a brief word about their loss, begin the discussion with words like. . .

"While most of us know some of the emotions of grief like sadness, loneliness, anger, fear, and guilt, we also experience grief physically. Often, bereaved people express great concern about loss of appetite, sleeplessness, and the lack of energy to participate in any activities or exercise. Tonight, I want us to talk about some of these challenges and learn from each other about how to manage these issues.

- What have been some of your biggest challenges with eating? What are you doing about these challenges?

- How have you been sleeping and how does this differ from how you slept before your loved one's death?

- How have your exercise habits changed since your loved one's death? Are there some things you think you would like to try?

For Reflection. . .

What are some of the ways your physical well-being has been affected by your own experiences with loss? Do you think these are typical of most people in bereavement? Why or why not?

_____
_____
_____
_____
_____
_____
_____
_____

Only a qualified professional should suggest a bereaved person is depressed

Make sure to address the relationship of these factors to full-blown clinical depression. Only a qualified professional should suggest that a bereaved person is depressed, but always keep in mind that changes in physical well-being can be symptomatic of depression. Work with people in the group individually to assess for depression if that is your expertise, or be ready to refer people to qualified support for an evaluation.

Bereaved people should be reminded to get a complete physical examination. Unless there is a pressing problem necessitating an earlier appointment, I recommend that bereaved people get a check-up two or three months after a loved one's death since this allows the "dust to settle."

Group Idea 4: When Guilt Consumes Us

For bereaved people, guilt usually comes from a false sense that the bereaved person *should* have been able to affect a different outcome (*should* and *ought* are always big components of this). Guilt is an unreasonable emotion, in that the one who feels guilty most often could have done nothing different to change the circumstances or to have made a better decision with the information that was known. To get the discussion started, ask: "When in your grief do you find yourself most consumed by guilt and regret, a sense that you should have or could have done something different?"

For follow-up questions, try these:

- In what ways has your guilt gotten better or worse since your loved one's death?

- What are the strategies you find most help with your guilt?

- How have your family and friends supported you as you grapple with guilt? Have they tried to talk you out of it or have they allowed you to experience this part of grief's emotion?

Before the meeting ends, make sure to give participants an opportunity to discuss some of their own coping strategies.

Group Idea 5: Dealing With Advice and Expectations

One of the hardest experiences for people in grief is to deal with the unrealistic expectations and the unsolicited advice offered by well-meaning friends and family members. Here are some questions to get your group talking about the advice and expectations of others:

- What is the worst advice anyone has given you so far in your grief? What is the best advice you've been given?

- How are your closest friends and family members supporting you in your grief? What do you wish they would do differently?

- What expectations do you have of yourself in grief or feel that other people have of you (ie get over this more quickly, get back to being your old self, etc.)

Your group members will likely have some very good ideas for dealing with the expectations and unwanted advice from others. Give them a chance to share their ideas. Some will have found the best way to deal with such issues is through humor: "Thank you for all the

Bereaved people get lots of free advice. A lot of it is worth about what they pay for it!

money you are saving me by not having to visit a therapist!" Others will simply ignore the advice of others, even though they may be gracious when it is offered.

Provide pens and paper or thank-you cards. Invite your group members to choose the person they feel has been most supportive to them in their grief. Ask them to write a simple note of gratitude, expressing one or two positive ways this person has been supportive and thanking them for their helpfulness. Encourage group members to be specific and then invite two or three group participants to share their letters with the rest of the group. Group members can either mail the letters to the addressee or find other ways to communicate their gratitude.

Group Idea 6: Dealing With Fear

Fear is most certainly one of the most common emotions expressed by people in grief. The leading models of the bereavement process suggest that the source of the fear is most often either a sense of helplessness regarding how to get along now that the loved one has died or from a heightened sense of the bereaved's own mortality and anxiety surrounding his or her own death.

Help your group participants learn to say thank you—for all the kindness they have received

With bereaved people, normalizing the fear is important. Hearing a supportive person say that fear is commonly experienced by people in grief goes a long way to mitigating its effects. Because fear is so common among the grieving, you can assume the presence of fear by asking a question like, "Of all the things that scare you about this experience, what do you suppose you fear the most?" Frequently, assuming the presence of fear helps the grieving person feel okay about expressing his fear.

Remind the griever that fears often relate to the important work of learning to live in a whole new world. One widow expressed this well when she reported, "I don't know how I will ever get by without him; he did everything for me."

Helping the bereaved discover the things that he/she does well and helping with "problem solving" can be useful techniques. For example, for a person who has never balanced a checkbook, help him create a plan with small, steps such as: 1) get your checkbook and statement; 2) ask at your bank if someone could help you the first time; 3) get familiar with the statement, etc.

It is also important to recognize that many bereavement-related fears are really fear of the unknown. If a bereaved person is afraid to be alone in the house, encourage a thorough security check. Many police departments have volunteer corps that will make a home security assessment at no cost.

Bereavement also raises concerns about one's own mortality. In her book, *Grief: The Mourning After*, Catherine M. Sanders writes, "Death anxiety is higher during bereavement than at other times," causing the bereaved to sometimes feel closer to that inevitable experience because of what he/she has seen. A thorough physical examination a few months after a loved one's death is good to discover how the grieving person's body is responding to the stress of grief. But it has an added benefit of helping to alleviate fears about physical health and concerns about getting the same disease that killed the deceased.

Bereaved people may fear that they "are not doing this right." A sense of hopelessness often grows out of the fear that "I'll never live through this." Participation in a support group of people who are learning to manage their grief-related fear is a valuable experience. Here, the bereaved often learn coping strategies and encounter others with similar experiences, thereby normalizing their own fears and minimizing the fear of "losing one's mind."

Bereavement groups are wonderful places for people to learn that they can live again

Remember that anxiety disorders existing before the loved one's death will most often be magnified by bereavement, so consultation with or referral to the mental health professional who is supervising the person's care is imperative. And while not likely, bereavement can give way to new clinical anxiety disorders for which a combination of counseling and medication proves useful.

Significant experiences with fear after a loved one's death are common for people in bereavement. The support and encouragement of professionals and volunteers are important aids to healing during this period.

Note: This is an especially good topic for consideration when a major holiday approaches while your group is meeting. For example, if you have a group that begins the first week of November, you'll want to address this topic at the second or third meeting, and promise at the first meeting, "since Thanksgiving, Christmas, Hannukah, New Years, etc. are just around the corner, we'll be talking about dealing with holidays in grief at our meeting on November ___. I hope you will plan to join us that night."

You can introduce the topic with words like,

> "Holidays and other important occasions are some of the most difficult days in grief, especially during the first year or two. Tonight we're going to be talking about ways to manage the hard times these special days bring to our lives. Holidays in grief are hard for a couple of reasons. First, holidays are filled with sentiment. We are bombarded by sights, sounds, and smells of the holiday. These clues tell us in unmistakable terms: "The holidays are here.""

Lead your group to make plans for managing the holidays

> "In the second place, holidays remind us of relationships. Whether the relationship with our loved one was good, bad, or some mixture of both, we collide with the reality that we are now alone. While families gather for celebration, we realize that our family now feels very incomplete. Some have not celebrated a birthday in many years without this person. Anniversaries are especially painful after our mate dies. Holidays are all about relationships and we have said goodbye to a very important person."

Here are some questions that will help your group talk about holiday plans and ways to manage grief on special days:

- Which holidays/special days do you most dread since your loved one died?

- What were your favorite activities for holidays/special days? How are those altered now with his/her death?

- If you have already lived through a holiday or special day in your grief, what was it like and how did you get through it?

Take a few minutes near the end of your meeting time to offer these ideas about handling the holidays:

◆ Acknowledge that grieving on special days and holidays is painful. Pretending that this holiday will be like those in the past is not realistic.

◆ Take care of your physical well-being. Good nutrition, rest, and exercise are important in all parts of grief but especially during the extra stresses of special days

◆ Make a plan. The special day is often as bad in the "dreading" as in the living. Having a plan for where to go and what to do will lessen the anxiety.

◆ Find someone to help during the season of special days. Consider volunteering to feed homeless people at Thanksgiving. At Easter, try volunteering to usher at church or provide some other ministry of service. Offering to become a "buddy" at a nursing home is always welcome.

Group Idea 8: Saying Goodbye to the Group

Saying goodbye is never easy, and for the group members who have become a community of support, the last meeting comes as a bittersweet experience. The following ideas will help as the "formal" group comes to a close:

◆ The end of the group does not have to mean we will never see each other; encourage group members to maintain contact with those they have become especially close to during the group

◆ A balloon launch can be an especially powerful way to close the group time. Secure helium and balloons at a party store or florist and make sure to get a few extra balloons since some always pop when inflated or when written on. Have group members write a special memory or goodbye message on the balloon with permanent felt-tip markers. Then, join in a circle, invite group members to share something special they are taking from the group, and release the balloons together. You will be amazed at the silence as participants—adults and children alike—quietly watch the balloons float upward until out of sight.

The real success of a group is getting people together to support each other

- If the group participants want, let them plan a potluck for the final meeting. If your group meets in borrowed facilities, make sure you learn what requirements must be met to serve food that is not professionally prepared and what arrangements must be made for clean up.

- Close the meeting with a unison reading like the "Farewell Blessing," found in the resource section at the end of this handbook. Standing in a circle while reading the words creates a very meaningful ceremony. Before the reading, invite group participants to share how they have been most touched by the group.

Even though this chapter has identified content to consider including in a bereavement support group, the real ingredient to success is getting people together to share their experiences. The group participants will almost always derive more help from actually attending the group than they will by any particular information the leader imparts.

Five

❧ Grief Groups for ❧ Children and Teens

Just a month after Javier's eleventh birthday, his father was killed in a car crash on the way to work. Javier, his mom, and his two sisters walked through the next few days in the numbness and shock common after such an unexpected death.

A couple of months after his father's death, however, Javier's teacher noticed he was continuing to miss school at least two days each week, usually because of vague complaints like a stomachache or headache. She told the school counselor that Javier was quite distracted even when he did attend, never really focusing on the assignment at hand. He almost never turned in homework and did poorly on tests, all behaviors that were quite different than what she had seen from this above-average fifth grader before his dad died.

Javier was a good candidate for a bereavement support group at school, his church, or community bereavement center. Like Javier, a child or teen who has experienced the death of a parent, grandparent, or sibling, could be helped immeasurably by a bereavement group designed with appropriate developmental characteristics in mind.

Since 1996, I have had the unique opportunity to hone practical strategies and techniques to support grieving kids through the "laboratory" of Pathways Volunteer Hospice in Long Beach, California. Our community volunteers have provided grief support to

Providing groups for children and teens acknowledges that their experiences with a loved one's death are real, too

hundreds of kids through community-based family bereavement programs and school-based groups.

Because of their developmental uniqueness, bereaved children and teenagers are different than their parents and other adults. While older teens might be expected to interact well in a support group that is mostly focused on talking and listening, younger kids will be most helped when their support groups combine art projects and games to help them understand and express the experiences of bereavement. Interestingly, games and art often become the means for children *to talk* about their grief experiences.

Understanding Younger Children in Grief

Leaders of groups for preschoolers and younger elementary aged children must understand that for this age group, death is a vaguely-grasped concept. The death of a primary caregiver or a person with whom the child interacts daily will greatly impact a young child, while the death of a neighbor or distant relative can be expected to have little impact. As children move past the toddler years, a support group becomes a practical possibility. I have colleagues who lead groups for children as young as 3, even though groups at Pathways generally include children in kindergarten and older.

For preschoolers and younger children, death and grief can only be grasped vaguely

For Reflection. . .

What are your first memories of loss as a child? A pet? A grandparent? A treasured possession?

_____

_____

_____

How did your family acknowledge the loss and help you work through your grief?

_____

_____

_____

What do you think your family did well in helping you with grief? Wat do you wish your family would have done differently?

_____

_____

_____

A child's concept of death changes rapidly as she grows. Very young children tend to view death as a magical "here yesterday, gone now, back tomorrow" kind of way, so the death of a loved one is not seen as permanent. What disturbs a young child most is disruption in his routine of eating, sleeping, and playing—so helping caregivers restore routine as quickly as possible is essential to a young child's healthy resolution of loss.

Professional and volunteer support people must help parents and other caregivers realize that young children sense the changes in their family after a loved one dies, even if no one tells them directly. A child who is not told the truth may conclude that the tears and chaos are her own fault.

By the time a child is in school, the notion of death permanence might be taking root, although you can never be sure at this age. As early as second grade, children are exposed in school science units to the concept of a life cycle and kids this age are certainly beginning to understand that living things die. Children learn that living things die, and that dead things stay dead.

Group leaders and support persons must always remember the conflicting messages young children receive about death from the culture. Television heroes are killed in one show only to magically reappear in the next episode. Baby boomers grew up watching the coyote meet his end every time he encountered *The Roadrunner*, only to magically reappear in the next episode.

The emphasis given to Halloween in our culture also plays havoc with a young child's concept of death. One kindergartener with whom I worked had ghoulish nightmares. On examination, the parents discovered this little girl's classroom was filled with images of ghosts, skeletons, and goblins. Each morning, her teacher led the class as they sang, "Good morning to the witches. . .ghosts. . .skeletons." The same school group sang a song about "skeletons dancing in the closet," which could be a most alarming concept for a six-year old whose grandmother died earlier in the year.

Grief groups for young children help them wrap their hands around unspeakable experiences. A group might be the only place a youngster can discuss death and learn positive ways to cope with it.

Children often receive conflicting messages about death and loss from the media, their friends, and family

As children grow, they gradually come to understand death as permanent, however much they may wish otherwise. However, two key issues arise as children move through the elementary school years. First, children between about six and ten tend to see death as the result of specific behavior, so they often see death as punishment for specific deeds. This perspective of "cause and effect" might lead a child to believe that he caused the death of the loved one, creating a sense of false guilt.

Like many nine-year olds, Brandon got in trouble for talking in the classroom and had been repeatedly warned by his teacher. When the behavior persisted, his teacher called home to report the problem to Brandon's parents. The next morning, shortly after arriving at work, Brandon's dad died of a massive heart attack. In the days and weeks that followed, all Brandon could think of was that his behavior and the teacher's call to his dad had caused the heart attack, consuming him with guilt.

Don't be surprised if older children exhibit an unquenchable thirst for details about the death

A second issue for children in this age group has to do with their thirst for details about the death. During these years, many children are fascinated with gore. A morbid preoccupation may appear, especially focused on the details of how, when, and where the deceased died. Children in this age group might desire to know more about the condition of the body than some family members are willing to discuss.

Though these questions tend to appear shortly after the death, they may surface again in a bereavement support group, especially if the child did not feel he got an adequate answer earlier. Be aware that in a group, the preoccupation with the details can escalate as children ask each other to describe what they saw and how their special someone died.

The best tactic in a group setting is to acknowledge the need to know and talk about ways to get questions answered. Remind the children often that one person's graphic description of the way his dad died can be enormously upsetting to another child in the same group.

Engaging Children in Groups

Effective bereavement support groups for children emphasize active learning, and the possibilities are almost endless. As you plan an activity, think through in advance how much time might be required to play the game, create the project, and discuss the experience. While you will want to plan realistically, always have one "fall-back" idea in case a project does not go as planned or you find yourself with too much time at the end of the group session.

While I have used these activities with a diversity of child groups, give some thought to the specific age group with which you are working and think through what might or might not work with the individual children in your group.

Pastels and water colors are excellent art media choices for older children and teens. You run little risk of damaging furniture, flooring, and clothes. Using the same media with young children without a smock and floor coverings, however, invites disaster.

In the first meeting or two of the group, you may find it difficult to predict how the children will respond. As you get to know the kids, however, you will find it easier and easier to anticipate how the activity will unfold.

Do yourself a favor—be sure your art media matches the age group of the children!

Here are some ideas to actively engage children in exploring their grief and learning positive coping strategies.

Dead Plant—Show children two potted plants of the same type, one live one and one dead one. Ask the children to help you describe the differences. Explain that death is what happens when a living thing doesn't work anymore, and that no amount of food or water can make it alive again. Help the children touch and smell the two plants and describe the differences. A good way to transition to a discussion of grief is by asking, "Has anything or anyone in your family ever died? Tell us about it. How did you find out it/he/she died? What was that like/How did you feel about it?"

Leaf Collage—Provide leaves in various colors, textures, and shapes or lead the children outside to gather them. Let the children touch and describe the leaves and help them contrast how the recently picked, green leaves feel different than the brown, dead ones. If you have access to leaves in fall colors, help them see that some dead leaves are actually quite beautiful. Provide paper and glue to the children so they can create a leaf collage.

Gingerbread Emotions—Using cookie cutters, let children trace a gingerbread person and agree on a color code for emotions (like red for anger and blue for sadness.) Color the person according to where the emotion is most keenly felt. This activity allows the group leader to affirm natural emotional experiences in grief and to allow children to compare how they feel with other children's feelings. Group leaders should watch for signals a child would benefit from individual intervention. Art that does not seem age appropriate, children who scribble angrily on the page, and kids who seem disengaged from the entire process provides clues that further evaluation is warranted.

Drawing—When children create pictures, they unlock a part of the brain that simply cannot be accessed with words alone. Almost any theme can provide an opportunity for children to draw, but here are a few examples of "invitations to draw" you can make with the children in a bereavement support group:

For children and adults, art often helps tell the story mere words can never fully capture

- ◆ Draw a picture of a favorite memory you have with the person who died

- ◆ Draw a picture of anger, guilt, fear, or some other emotion

- ◆ Draw a picture of how your family looks now

- ◆ Draw a picture of your favorite place to go together

- ◆ Draw a picture of your favorite holiday

When the children have finished drawing their pictures, invite them to tell the group about what they have drawn. Engage the children in discussion; when a child says Christmas was her favorite holiday with her grandma, ask her to "tell us more" or ask, "What did you most like about spending Christmas with your grandma?" As the group session proceeds, you will also have opportunities to talk with the children about how things are different now, about the changes that have come about because of the death of their special person.

Do not try your hand at art therapy by attempting to see "deeper meanings" in the colors or themes that are chosen. In support groups for children, focus on normalizing the experience of grief, providing practical instruction on managing grief, and creating a climate where a child is free to express the range of grief's experiences. Art becomes a way to move toward all of those goals.

Memory Box—Having one place to deposit the memorabilia from a loved one's life is a huge help to grieving children (and the rest of the family, as well). In our family bereavement support program at Pathways, parents, children, and teens all create a personal memory box in their respective groups on the same night.

Small wooden boxes can be bought from a craft store and decorated with paint, decorative appliqués, or glued photographs. One nine-year old decorated the memory box of her musician father with musical notes and photographs of him conducting an orchestra. Inside, she put additional photographs, a letter she wrote to him, and a copy of a CD he had recorded.

Memory boxes help children—and their parents—tell about the symbols they most treasure

For Reflection. . .

What other activity and discussion ideas do you have for working with children in grief?

_____
_____
_____
_____
_____
_____
_____
_____
_____
_____
_____

Beginning a week or two in advance, we encourage parents to take their family to the craft store to select a box and any decorative media they might like to have. Sometimes just wandering around the store as a family looking for appropriate symbols creates important sharing time. Our group leaders always have a supply of extra boxes, decorative stickers, pens, and paint on hand.

While the children are creating their memory boxes, the group leader can engage the children with questions like

- What are you making?

- What does that mean?

- How did you come to choose that color?

- What will you put in your box?

Games—You can use many of the everyday board games children play to help them talk about loss, change, and emotions. *Chutes and Ladders* for younger children help them see the inevitability of making great progress, only to "slide" nearly back to the beginning. *Jenga* is especially useful for older children as the kids take turns removing wood blocks while trying to prevent the tower from falling.

With *Jenga*, I like to invite the children to share something about their loved one—a special memory, a favorite holiday, or a gift they treasure given by the person who died.

I recommend enlisting the help of one or two elementary teachers as consultants. A teacher who has taught several different age groups and who appreciates the developmental differences of kids is an excellent choice. If you do not have experience with children and art, invite an elementary art teacher to join your team—as either a consultant or a group facilitator.

Local school teachers can be invaluable in their advice and experience dealing with children. Enlist their help!

Understanding the Grieving Teenager

Adolescence is filled with changes—physical, emotional, cognitive, spiritual, and social. Major losses during these years creates havoc in a life filled with more transitions than most adults remember.

For Reflection. . .

What have you observed with grieving teenagers? Do you think your observations represent "typical grief" for adolescents?

_____
_____
_____
_____
_____
_____
_____

The teen years mark the period of transition from fully-dependent children to fully-functioning adults. Along the way, teens often become fairly disenchanted with their parents and many of the other adults around them. When death comes to a parent or primary caregiver during these years, the challenges are daunting. If the relationship was marked by conflict—as most parent-teen relationships are—you can expect guilt.

Adolescents are also known for believing they are invincible. To a teenager, death is something that happens for sure—but never to them, a friend, or a family member. This belief may be part of the underlying reason teens often exhibit the most dangerous risk-taking behaviors. Death in a close relationship shakes this feeling of invincibility and the teen's new task becomes discovering how to make sense of the new reality.

Group leaders with teens will want to be especially alert to the "quiet thinker," a student who often writes or draws by himself. Teens often become very introspective in grief and may experience bereavement philosophically. They may wonder why one person dies and another lives, why suffering and pain exist in the world, and what purpose there is to life after a loved person has died. Adolescence is marked by spiritual and philosophical questions; the death of a loved one only intensifies the quest.

Teens might become introspective and even philosophical. But this is part of the bereavement process for them

Teens often believe that their grief makes them different in the eyes of their peers, a huge challenge for adolescents. One of their greatest fears is that they somehow don't "fit in" with their group. Because a death makes them feel "different," many teens do not even want their friends notified that there has been a death in the family. Respect the teen's need to fit in and also provide strong support groups of other teens who are also bereaved.

Engaging Teens in Grief Groups

Anyone who has been asked to lead a teen grief group might be frightened. The older we get, the less we feel like we can meaningfully "connect" with teenagers. However, grieving teenagers desperately need the guiding hand of a caring adult. Knowing all "the answers" is not a prerequisite for helping grieving teens. Possessing a willingness to explore the depths of loss with teenagers who want to find their way is the most important characteristic. Here are some ideas for activities with grieving teens.

Food—An army marches on its stomach, we are told. More than with any other bereavement group, I believe teen groups function best in the presence of groceries! In fact, the most effective teen group I ever led was a 30-minute lunchtime group at a local high school. Out of necessity, the school counselors got together and bought pizza and soft drinks for the kids, knowing they only had 30 minutes between classes. Somehow pizza and soda helped break down walls and these kids shared intimately. Several weeks after the group concluded, one of the counselors told me she saw our group sitting together at a quiet out-of-the-way table having lunch together. Though they were part of a high school with 3,000 students and had not known each other before the group began, these students had become a healing community for each other.

Food might be just the missing ingredient in a teen bereavement group

"What We Think About Death" Discussion—Lead a discussion about how the teens' concept of death has changed. What did they used to believe about death that they no longer believe? What are some things now believed that did not used to be part of their "system?"

Picture Collage—Similar to the Leaf Collage activity suggested above for children, this activity engages teens in creating a mosaic of words and photos clipped from magazines into an artistic expression of grief. For the activity, you will want to have on hand a number of magazines (at least some with teen themes), art paper, scissors, and glue sticks.

You can lead the group to go any number of directions with this activity, depending on the concept you want to help grieving teens discover. Here are a few themes; you can either select one theme or invite teens to create collages with themes that most interest them.

  ◆ *Change/Transition.* Select pictures and words that portray change or transition Are they all good changes, bad changes, or some of both?

  ◆ *Memories.* Select pictures and words that remind you of the person who died? What were the factors that led you to choose these pictures? What were you thinking as you selected these words?

- *People*. Select pictures of a variety of people. How do the people in the pictures you have selected remind you of the different people who are or can be supportive to you in your grief.

Games—Playing *Jenga* with teens is especially helpful in getting a discussion started, and I like to use it as an "ice-breaker" at the first group meeting. As we go around the group taking turns pulling a block from the tower and trying to prevent its collapse, I ask participants to share a favorite memory, a holiday tradition, or a special gift received from the loved one.

After the tower collapses (as it always does!), I ask a group member to rebuild the tower *exactly* like it was. Usually, one participant will volunteer and begin to restack the blocks. A couple of rows into the reassembly, however, I stop him and point out that not every block is *exactly* where it was. Some are turned differently and I'll usually say something like, "I know that block was actually on the top row. . ." This is met with the complaint, "Well of course they're not exactly where they all were; that would be impossible." This admission gives us a chance to talk about the inevitability of change in grief.

Keeping a journal is a skill teens can develop that will serve them the rest of their lives

I then ask, "How do you think that might be kind of like life after someone we love dies?" Even though we rebuild our lives after loss, and the rebuilt life can be very good, our life is certainly not life with every "block" in the same place.

Writing—Teaching and modeling the keeping of a journal can be an especially useful strategy with grieving teens. Even teens who do not usually enjoy writing often embrace the idea of writing a poem or a story about their loss or about the person who died. Providing a simple spiral-bound notebook to teens is an important way to encourage the keeping of a journal. When asking teens to write, make sure to give them specific guidelines like the following "journal starters:"

- Today, I am thinking about the holiday when we. . .
- Today, I am thinking about when I first learned of the death. . .
- Today, I am thinking about the time we went. . .
- Today, I am thinking how grateful I am for. . .

- Today, I am thinking about how angry/guilty/sad/lonely/scared I am because. . .

- Today, I find the hardest part of this experience to be. . .

Remember that teens often *write* through their grief when they do not feel ready to *talk* it out. One mother was especially concerned because her 16 year old daughter would not discuss her father's death. At the urging of her own support group for widowed parents, the mom asked her daughter if she ever wrote about her dad. The daughter excitedly replied, "Oh, yeah, mom—would you like me to read you some of what I've written?" The mom later reported that she and her daughter sat up for hours reading and talking together about their grief.

Scrapbook—Even though the memory box idea in the children's activity section can be used with all ages, scrapbooks are a good alternative with teen group participants. A personalized scrapbook not only encourages teens to collect photos and other flat items in once place, but the scrapbook also provides a place to write stories and comments related to the teenager's grief. In my experience, teenage boys often are not interested in making a scrapbook, though you can always give them the choice.

Personal Shield—Create a personal "shield" or a "Coat of Arms" on a sheet of poster board or art paper. The facilitator can either have on hand a "shield" already traced and cut out, or the participants can be encouraged to simply design their own. Encourage the group members to divide their shield into at least four or five segments and draw a picture or write words that remind them of people or memories they find supportive.

Encourage the artistic side of grieving teens. Your compliments will help negate their self-criticism

Some of the pictures we've seen people put into their shield segments are: a Bible, stick-figure representation of family, a school building/classroom picture, a church, and two friends sitting together having lunch. Either way, having a sample shield with the facilitator's personal support symbols is helpful to show the teens. Encourage creativity—whatever seems supportive to the bereaved person is fair-game here! Perhaps because of the military theme of a "shield," adolescent and pre-adolescent boys seem to really like this activity.

Sharing Music—Teenagers sometimes seem defined by the music to which they listen! Angi Waller, one of the best volunteer group leaders with teens I know, invites teenagers to bring a CD to one session. She tells the teens to bring music that remind them of the special person who died or is especially meaningful to them as they adjust to grief.

During the session, teens take turns playing their favorite music a portable stereo Angi brings to the group. As the music is played, Angi leads the teens in talking about how music engages a different part of us than talk alone, and how music can help us remember special times.

Discussing Movies —My wife and I have a running joke that every movie we see has a death theme or sub-plot. With tongue only partly "in cheek," I sometimes say a death is required to make a good story! Since teens know popular movies, capitalize on this awareness to talk about the death and loss themes in popular films.

For Reflection. . .

What other activity and discussion ideas do you have for working with teens in grief?

_____
_____
_____
_____
_____
_____
_____
_____
_____
_____
_____

If you aren't sure what movies teens are watching, ask them!

Learning From Our Losses: A One-Session Grief Support Experience

Family and community schedules sometimes make it unlikely that a multi-session support group will be effective. Moreover, the resources of trained group leaders might make a one-time group a good choice, even if repeated on a quarterly basis. Hosting a one-session grief support experience like *Learning from Our Losses* can be a great way to gauge community interest in a support group for children and/or teens.

Of course, bereavement is not an instantly-resolved experience. One danger of a one-session group is that some families might infer that children can attend a three-hour "class" and be "over it." Those who work with grieving children and teens understand that nothing could be further from the truth.

Nevertheless, a one-session group can be very helpful for children and teens, especially when they are trying to learn how to cope with the death of a grandparent, a classmate, or friend. Here are a few steps to organizing a *Learning from Loss* bereavement support experience for kids.

First, decide the key concepts you want to expose children to in a one-session group. Covering three or four ideas in a couple of hours is a realistic goal. The emphasis in a one-session group needs to be on normalizing the experiences of grief and helping kids discover where they can look for support.

Here are a few ideas you can help children and teens grasp during a one-session experience and a suggested activity from this handbook.

Grief will never be resolved in a single session. But we can provide tools and ideas for the journey

- ◆ Grief is a natural part of life, always to be expected after any transition including a loved one's death (Leaf Collage/ PictureCollage)

- ◆ Grief affects every part of us—emotional, physical, mental, spiritual, and social (Gingerbread Emotions)

- ◆ Memories help us heal (Memory Box, Scrapbook, Sharing Music, Drawing activities)

- ◆ Grief is best resolved when shared with supportive people (Personal Shield, Picture Collage)

Consider beginning the one-session support experience with a game like *Chutes and Ladders* or *Jenga* (discussed above). You can end the experience with a family activity or picnic.

Single-session grief support experiences provide a compelling introduction to multi-session models. If a parent, child, or teen is reticent to participate in a longer-term group, a single experience might help them "test the waters."

Single-session groups can also be vital for helping families begin a dialogue. I have been amazed at the numbers of families I meet who never really talk about a loved one's death, share memories, or interact about the experiences of grief. Participating in a support group together often unlocks the door simply because of the narrow focus of a two-hour family group.

Do not overlook the possibility of a single session group focused on one activity. A creative title like *Scrapbooking our Memories* can engage children, teens, and adults in a one-session experience focused on making a scrapbook of stories, photos, etc. A scrapbooking store or consultant might be willing to underwrite some costs by providing materials or staff at a discount. The store benefits because participants only start their album; they will undoubtedly want additional materials to complete it.

Providing Tools for Life

Death, loss, and transition form an important backdrop to life. Though the death of a loved one that brought teens or children into your group might be the first significant loss they have experienced, it will certainly not be the last.

Whether through a multi-session bereavement group or a single session experience, one of the values of bereavement support is that participants learn healthy coping skills for whatever losses they experience. Facing the death of a loved one can be a life-enriching, life-affirming experience. Your group provides positive tools for kids that create a lifetime of value.

My Reflections. . .

_Pausing to reflect helps
nourish the spirit and
provide vision for the
future_

Six

⤳ Complicated Grief ⤳
in the Support Group

Jackie was 32-years old when she attended her first grief group meeting. Her husband of three years had completed suicide four months earlier, and she was searching for help in understanding her experience. When she finally spoke at her first meeting, everyone knew of her ambivalent feelings toward her husband. Theirs had been a rocky marriage anyway, and his suicide had put a capstone on their relationship. Her anger and rage boiled out—"How could he do this to the kids and me? We were just starting to work things out. He had a great job, great friends—so much to live for."

Professional counselors regularly meet bereaved people who are not even aware that unresolved loss is behind their difficulties. People who attend grief groups are usually different. They recognize the power of their loss and they want tools, resources, and people like them. They are usually *eager* to "move on." But some factors can complicate their grief.

People with complicated losses may need both your group and the individualized help of a skilled professional

For Reflection. . .

What most concerns you about having someone like Jackie in a group you lead? Are there some issues about which you want to learn more?

_____
_____
_____
_____
_____

How the Death Occurred. Generally, expected deaths from natural causes tend to lead to less complication in the bereavement process than deaths that were the result of a sudden accident, murder, or suicide.

When death occurred by violent means—a car crash or a homicide for example—bereaved people often struggle with questions about the victim's fears and last thoughts, wondering what was going through her mind in those closing moments of life. Perhaps this is why we are gratified to hear after such a death, "He never knew what hit him" or "The coroner said she died instantly."

Especially in groups that focus on a particular traumatic loss—families of murder victims and survivors after a suicide, for example—participants will likely want to talk about what they imagine the last moments were like. I have found allowing them to express their fears and concerns about their loved one's death is instrumental in helping them heal.

Listen for what people describe—the event of the death or the loss in the relationship

Group leaders should be aware that there is a distinct difference between the response to trauma and the experiences of grief. While well beyond the scope of this handbook, trauma is a stress reaction resulting from a shocking, surprising death. Trauma victims may continually re-experience the event through flashbacks which often interfere with sleep.

People whose loved one died traumatically commonly avoid the place where the death occurred. Carol's son was killed in a motorcycle crash only six blocks from their home. Even though the most direct route to the supermarket, Carol's temple, and her place of work was through the intersection where the accident occurred, Carol chose to go more than two miles out of her way to avoid that corner.

Traumatized people often experience anxiety over the event happening again so they may appear to be on "high alert." In telling their story, the details they share tend to focus on the *event* of the death rather than the *relationship* that was lost. If this person attends a bereavement group, he will repeatedly tell the details of the death rather than talk deeply about his memories of life with the deceased and what he most misses about her.

Even after witnessing a horrific death, most trauma survivors experience a gradual lessening of these symptoms, usually within a month or so. Those whose trauma symptoms continue to impair their day-to-day functioning longer than a month may be diagnosed with Post-Traumatic Stress Disorder (PTSD), usually requiring the intervention of a trained mental health professional.

Expectation of Death. Closely connected to how the deceased died is what the bereaved person *believed* about the likelihood of death. The husband of a cancer patient in the advanced stages of the disease who cared for his wife at home on hospice care and daily watched the decline would have a far different view of the death than the mother whose son was killed in a carjacking.

Remember, though, that what a family *believed* about a terminal illness is more significant than what the doctors *said* about the prognosis. Regardless of what they are told, some people expect their loved one to recover until he takes his last breath. These bereaved people might be more like the person for whom there was no warning of the coming death.

The utter shock of an unexpected death usually delays people getting started in the process of readjusting their lives after loss; they just can't believe it happened. Sometimes, this feeling persists for many weeks.

Unexpected deaths carry much shock—and often delay the experiences with bereavement

Age of the Deceased. Though "age at death" is relative, be sure there is a pervasive belief in our society about who is "supposed to die" and who is not. The younger the person, the more tragically our society tends to view his death. Children, we believe, are not supposed to die before their parents. We wonder about how, with all of the advances in medical technology, diseases in children are not cured. We reel at the notion that a four-year old dies of leukemia, and the parents acutely feel that sense of injustice.

On the other end of the age spectrum, the adult children of a 95-year old Alzheimer's patient may be scolded by their well-meaning friends for expressing sadness at the death of their parent. "How can you grieve for her when she is so much better off?" might be the unhelpful words spoken (or implied) to these grieving people. These bereaved people need the group to reassure them that grief is normal, regardless of "how long we had our parents."

Virtually everyone who attends a bereavement support group will feel that life with their loved one was cut short, whether that relationship was marked in days or in decades. The mother of a baby who dies from Sudden Infant Death Syndrome longs to hold the little one in her arms and grieves for a future cut short. In the same way, the new widow wishes for more time with her husband, even though they had been married for 60 years.

Compromised Support System. If there is poor communication, substance addiction, or abuse in a family, the bereavement group may be the only place grieving people really feel free to express their thoughts and feelings. Earlier, I indicated that a good grief group becomes a community for bereaved people, and participants who come from families with serious dysfunction benefit even more from a good group.

Today's families are also often scattered geographically. The adult children may live hundreds of miles from their newly widowed parent. Even though they call regularly, they do not visit often. At best, phone calls rank a distant second place to personal presence.

The grief group might be the only place a person feels free to express the thoughts and feelings of their losses

Mobility limitations also cause many grieving people to feel "cut off" from the community. Perhaps fear of falling or becoming a crime victim keeps them home. Failing eyesight has perhaps ended their ability to drive.

I have frequently had group members for whom a neighbor or friend became their "wheels" to get them to and from groups, but I have also seen groups that start their own internal carpool to make sure everyone has a ride.

Undoubtedly, the natural support system—a healthy family or church group for example—is the best support for people in grief. When these connections are lacking or need to be supplemented by others who understand loss, however, the bereavement group becomes a precious lifeline.

Organic Mental Disorders. Regardless of how well you screen participants, you will periodically encounter group participants who have a long psychiatric history. Sometimes, these people are under professional care and their disease is well-controlled. For others, the loss that brought them to the group has magnified their illness and created a psychiatric crisis.

Some people with longstanding mental illnesses believe their issues are so advanced that only a highly trained therapist can work with them; they will tend to look elsewhere for a group, especially if you provide strong direction and leadership to your group.

This handbook is used by a variety of people from many backgrounds and with many different levels of training and experience. However, if you clearly say that the bereavement group is a mutual help group for education and support and not a therapy group, many with chronic mental health issues will look elsewhere for support.

Demystifying Depression in Grief

Perhaps the most common experience reported by people in grief is depression. Referred to by some as the "common cold of mental health disorders," depression can be expected to affect up to 20% of the population at some point in their lifetime.

All loss involves some level of sadness and yearning for the deceased, and this sadness is generally most prevalent in the early months after the loss. While these characteristics look like depression, strictly speaking, most of this is *reactive* depression rather than *biological* depression.

All loss involves some level of sadness—but this is clearly different than clinical depression

Even though some physicians routinely prescribe anti-depressant medication to their patients after a loss, the reactive depression most characteristic of bereavement does not respond to medication. In spite of the lack of effectiveness, some groups I have led had one-third of group participants who were taking an antidepressant prescription they were given soon after their loved one's death.

Virtually all grief includes *reactive* depression. An adaptive response, reactive depression follows losses of all kinds and frequently accompanies otherwise happy events. The post-holiday blues experienced by people is really reactive depression. After a period of high stress and intense adrenaline arousal, this depression is the body's way of giving itself time for recuperation while it goes into a "recovery mode."

After the death of a loved person or other significant loss, most people experience reactive depression. In other words, grief is most often characterized by deep sadness, loss of interest in pleasurable things, weight gain or loss, sleep disturbances, and the general malaise characteristic of clinical depression. Readers with a clinical background will recognize these symptoms as the primary criteria used to diagnose clinical depression. This depression is very real but it does not, at least initially, involve the chemical changes in the brain present with biological depression

Confusion abounds—both in professional and lay circles—about the best course of treatment for reactive depression. Under most circumstances, however, talking through or writing through the pain of grief helps, as does improving habits of exercise, nutrition, and rest.

Much recent research has also verified what people of faith have thought all along; participation in meaningful spiritual practices (like worship or prayer) also has a healing effect on reactive depression. Incidentally, these same factors also provide documented benefits for people with biological or clinical depression. For a more detailed discussion of this research, you can access the publications and web resources of the Center for Medicine and Religion at Duke University.

Listen for thoughts of one's own death or suicide; these clearly point toward clinical depression

Biological depression (technically called endogenous depression because it comes from inside the person) can also be present in people working through loss. Sometimes called a "chemical imbalance," these depressions are the visible symptoms of a change in the brain's chemistry.

For reasons that are not entirely understood, sometimes the brain fails to manufacture or reuse enough of its neurotransmitters, the chemical substances that carry messages from one brain cell to another. When the neurotransmitter Serotonin is too low, for example, depression in varying severity is a common result.

This depression is characterized by many of the same symptoms as a reactive depression, most commonly highlighted by a sad mood, extreme irritability, and loss of interest in the people, places, and activities that bring pleasure.

Clinically depressed people will also frequently have thoughts of their own deaths or even suicide, and usually suffer from very low self-esteem. These last two characteristics point to clinical depression rather than the reactive depression or extreme sadness of bereavement.

Now it is known that high levels of stress can reduce available Serotonin in the brain, so it makes sense that some reactive depressions can become full-blown chemical depressions. One reason to provide strong support for the experiences of grief is that this support usually reduces the stress of grieving, possibly preventing a full-blown biological depression.

Reactive depressions generally lift gradually as the grieving person does the hard work of grief. Expressing sadness, getting adequate rest, and allowing the body to "recover" from its emotional overload all work to heal this kind of depression. Encouraging the experiences of sadness related to the loss and providing a safe place to talk through the issues of grief seem to be the most helpful strategies to use. As this reactive depression gradually begins to lift, the bereaved person is reminded that while bereavement is far from over, the process is working.

If clinical depression is present, one of the newest classes of anti-depressant medication on the market, the SSRI (Selective Serotonin Reuptake Inhibitor) may prove clinically useful. Keep in mind however, that most of these drugs take weeks to build up enough concentration in the body to provide significant therapeutic benefits. And of course virtually no medication is without some side-effects. The potential side-effects for the SSRI's include gastric upset, loss of appetite, sleep disruption, and memory or concentration difficulties.

If your training or experience is limited, be sure to consult with a more experienced mental health professional

These side effects serve to magnify the grief experiences for many people, since these reactions are frequently part of the bereavement process already. In other words, prescribing anti-depressants prematurely, for people without a history of clinical depression, evidence of severe depression, or suicidal thoughts, often produce side effects well beyond any real therapeutic benefit. Many therapists, however, feel that people who have been treated successfully with medication for clinical depression in the past would be advised to begin medication therapy again after a significant loss.

In any case, if you are in doubt or if your clinical experience with depressed people is limited, make sure to consult with a more experienced mental health professional and encourage grieving people to talk with their physician or psychotherapist.

If you are a volunteer group leader, you may have difficulty knowing how and where to refer people to mental health services. The following ideas will help you make good referrals for people in your grief group who would benefit from professional mental health consultation.

Ask your supervisor. The person to whom you report will likely know of other resources in the community.

Consider the organization sponsoring your group. Many hospices, hospitals, and churches have counseling programs led by experienced professionals.

Ask group members for referrals. If members of your group indicate they are working with a therapist, ask them privately if they would be willing to give you that person's name and contact information.

Screen therapists. Your reputation is on the line when you refer a group member to a psychotherapist in the community. Phone the office of a therapist, indicate to her that you lead a bereavement support group and that you would like to talk to her about referring group members to her practice. I ask if this is a good time to talk or if later would be better; the therapist might have only three minutes before the next client arrives.

Screen professionals to whom you would refer group members

When approached this way, you will find most mental health professionals are delighted to answer your questions about their practice, style of therapy, or other points of interest because they realize you can be an important referral source. Questions to ask when you talk with the therapist include

* How long have you been in practice?

* What are your areas of clinical specialty or special interest?

* What do you believe about bereavement and the role of support groups?

* What are your payment options? Do you have a plan to help individuals or families who have limited resources or no insurance?

Make sure that you feel this person is approachable and that you find it easy to converse with him or her. If you have difficulty connecting, he will not return your calls within one business day, or she does not seem to want to answer your questions, move on to the next person on your list. People you would refer to this practice would find it no easier to get help here and grieving people do not need the extra stress.

Complicated Grief in the Group

Practically every loss includes some complicating factors. Perhaps the family relationship or the survivor's relationship with the deceased was markedly strained. Perhaps the death came suddenly and without warning, involved severe trauma, or came to a young person in "the prime of life." You may have people who attend your grief group as the first step in resolving a loss they encountered many years ago.

If you remember your group's goals, you do not have to be overly concerned about working with people with somewhat complicated grief experiences. Your goal is to create a community where people feel freedom to express the range of experiences with grief and to learn how better to manage those experiences.

Jackie, whose story began this chapter, would benefit most from being with people who allowed her to express the unique mixture of thoughts and feelings she had about her husband's death. A group leader who sees to it that her bereavement support group provides that kind of support has gone a long way to helping Jackie find healing in her loss.

My Reflections. . .

Pausing to reflect helps
nourish the spirit and
provide vision for the
future

Seven

Help! My Group is Sinking!

Jeff Turner, an experienced funeral director is also a veteran seafarer! According to Jeff, if a sailboat gets caught in a storm, "Dream of land and do everything you can to get there!"

But if the captain cannot get safely to land ahead of the storm, his sole job becomes protecting his ship, crew, and passengers from the storm by "heaving to." A smart sailor turns the bow into the waves, battens down the hatches, locks the helm in place, gets inside the cabin, and rides out the storm.

Whatever else happens, the captain does not want the boat sideways to the storm—unless he has a sturdy life jacket. A boat sideways to the storm is at a far greater risk of capsizing, destroying the vessel, and risking the lives of everyone on board.

You will not lead bereavement groups long before you will experience storms. If not managed well, the minor "squalls" that inevitably arise will send your group's "boat" right to the bottom of the ocean!

If not effectively handled, the minor "squalls" can become major storms in a grief group

Poor Marketing

The best bereavement group is of no value if people cannot find it. Many groups founder despite effective leadership and a community full of grieving people. Failure to thrive often arises just because no one knew about the group.

You can take several steps to avoid this "storm." If your group is sponsored by a hospice, church, senior center, or other organization with bereaved people among its constituents, you have a great starting point. However, simply placing an announcement in the organization's newsletter is unlikely to yield a huge influx of group participants.

Distribute an Informational Flyer. Create a flyer that includes dates, times, locations, and sponsors. Tell how the group is structured and what participants can expect to learn or how they will benefit from being in the group. Remember, if a person has never participated in a bereavement support group, she does not know what to expect or why she should attend. Tell her.

Take copies of the flyer to funeral homes, hospice offices, hospital pastoral care and social work offices, senior centers, and to any other professionals who would know people in need of your group. Though more time-consuming, you will find a personal visit to the organization pays richer dividends than simply mailing out a letter and flyers. A sample flyer is included in the resource section at the end of this handbook.

Let the newspaper help you promote your group.

Follow-Up. Just because you dropped off a few flyers at the hospice office four weeks ago does not mean anyone remembers today. Make a follow-up phone call to let the bereavement coordinator know how the group is going and that you still have room for more participants. Do the same thing with faith communities, funeral homes, and others you contacted at the beginning.

Notify the Newspaper. In the health or lifestyle section, most major newspapers publish a calendar listing support groups. The section editor will tell you how to submit information. Do not overlook the smaller community newspapers that are published weekly, as well. Getting your announcement in these smaller papers is usually much easier and community members almost always read these informal community papers.

Expect Growth. Few grief groups start out with a standing-room-only crowd. Two or three at the beginning can grow to your optimum size of six to ten. Be patient and expect growth to occur as people learn of your group.

Use Word of Mouth. Unless your group is closed to new participants, encourage the current participants to invite bereaved friends. A good group's best advertising is the people who are already being helped. Ask your group members what they like best about the group and encourage them to tell their friends.

Ineffective Leadership

Ineffective leadership will sink a group faster than any other factor. Effective group leaders seem to share some particular characteristics.

Focus on who comes. One reason a group works is because people realize their story is important. The most important people in your group—whether it is three or ten—are the people who attend. I have seen many group leaders who voice disappointment to the group that "more did not come tonight," and that always causes group members to feel their presence was unimportant. If there is more room in the group, briefly say so. Otherwise, affirm the courage of those who attend and focus your attention on their growth.

Follow-up. People want to know their part in the group is important. Group members seem to appreciate a brief phone call after they attend their first meeting. Simply thank them for coming and ask if there are any questions about the group. If one of your "regulars" misses more than a meeting or two, you will want to follow up to learn if illness or some other factor is keeping her away.

Take Charge. If you do not lead the group, your most vocal group member will! Do not surrender the group's welfare to whoever makes the most noise. People in need of a grief group usually hope someone will lead them through the chaos and confusion of early bereavement, the premise behind the title of this handbook, *Guiding People Through Grief*.

Asking at the beginning of a group meeting, "So, what would you like to talk about tonight?" is a proven recipe for disaster. The suggestions for group content in Chapter Four will provide better alternatives to get a group meeting started. Good leaders plan a question or two to begin the group.

If you don't take charge of the group, your most vocal group member will!

Every group has them and nearly every group leader dreads them: the "problem people" who make group leadership an extra challenge! These people do not intend to make life hard for the group leader, but their actions often cause problems. Here are ways to handle some of the more persistent problem characters in bereavement support groups.

Helpful Henrietta. Henrietta always has an idea to share about how she got through grief, but unfortunately, Henrietta assumes everyone else should get through grief the same way. Planning ahead can ease this problem. Make sure you talk with your group about why unsolicited advice may not be useful (see the discussion of Ground Rules in Chapter Four.)

During the group meetings, remind participants that most people in grief need a place to tell the story. Help them see that advice-giving often stops the story in mid-sentence and frequently creates in the mind of a newly bereaved person the notion that he/she is "not doing this right." If these reminders to the entire group are not enough to encourage "Henrietta" to keep her advice to herself, simply take her aside at the end of a group meeting and tactfully—but firmly— explain the problem.

Monopolizing Monty. You will not lead groups long before Monty will show up. He loves groups with non-directive leaders. You will know Monty by two key characteristics: 1) the tendency to take far longer than anyone else in describing his situation, and 2) the tendency to make a comment after everyone else's remarks—often with words of advice the other group members did not request.

You must deal firmly with Monty. Take him aside after a group meeting and point out what you have noticed. Ask him not to speak twice until everyone else has spoken once.

During the group, when you ask a question or ask folks to respond to something another group member has said, add something like, "Let us hear from some of you who have not had a chance to talk yet. . ."

Side-talking Sally. Sally is present in every group and she drives leaders crazy. She carries on conversations with a neighbor, often while another group member is talking. Besides being incredibly rude

Problem characters are not trying to be disruptive; they just need direction from the group leader

to the person who "has the floor," her behavior distracts other group members who want to hear.

Deal firmly with this by simply saying, "In order for everyone to hear, we can only talk one at a time. The side conversations make it difficult to hear, especially for those who have difficulty hearing anyway. I know it might remind you of first grade again, but it is important that we only talk one at a time." If the behavior does not change, you will need to talk to the offending group member privately.

Quiet Quentin. Every group has someone who seems content to sit and absorb rather than participate in the discussion. Many newcomers to bereavement groups say very little during the first or second meeting they attend.

Quentin may be quiet because there are so many of the other characters described in the group and the leader is doing little to direct the group process. If your group gets larger than a dozen or so in attendance, you will also find more than your share of Quentins.

However, Quentin may just need to be encouraged to talk. After he has attended several group meetings without saying much, try encouraging him with words like, "Quentin, we've not heard much from you; how about a penny for your thoughts. . ." or "Quentin, what do you think about this issue?"

Quiet members need permission to remain quiet, but they also need encouragement to talk

Group leaders always walk a fine line with quiet members. Groups work because no one is forced to say anything, and you will want to affirm this value. Perhaps a group member feels she has nothing valuable to add to the group discussion, so your encouragement might be all it will take for him to talk more openly. With a little encouragement, your Quiet Quentin might begin to share ideas that reflect the depth of thought and emotion characteristic of people who talk less.

Dysfunctional Darla. For this group participant, bereavement is just another problem in a litany of life's challenges. She was raised by abusive parents, had an alcoholic mate, possesses a long list of failed relationships, or has never had employment success. While our family and community relationships have a direct influence on how a person processes loss, people like Darla often need the guidance of a mental health professional to deal with the string of family and personality issues present in her life.

Frequently this person becomes a Monopolizing Monty because the grief group becomes a place to share all these problems with empathetic listeners.

Even if you have the training and experience to handle this person, the bereavement group is not the place; too much of the group's focus and energy is required, week in and week out. Work with Darla individually if that is your expertise or refer her to a family therapist or clinical psychologist. Chapter Six will help you make the best possible referrals.

Effective bereavement group leaders take on a role of "protector." For a group to become a safe community, leaders must assume a leadership role that assures everyone of an opportunity to tell his or her story without being subjected to unwanted advice, rude behavior, and a host of other problems that disrupt the group experience. Paying attention and addressing these difficult characters will go a long way to making your support group more effective for everyone attending.

Remember bereaved people may be completely oblivious to the behaviors that annoy leaders and other group members

All of these problems share similarity in how they are addressed. Problem behaviors often disappear as you remind everyone of the "group rules" participants agreed to when the group began. In a few cases, you will need to talk to group members privately about problems they are causing to the group process. Remember that bereaved people may be completely oblivious to the behaviors you notice, so always lace your comments with kindness and consideration.

Exhausted Leaders

Sixteenth century English poet John Donne is perhaps best known for his words, "No man is an island entire of itself. . ." Bereavement group leaders do well to remember that the work we do is difficult, demanding strong roots and the support of other people.

Taking care of yourself is paramount. Even seasoned bereavement group leaders can get caught up in the strain of hearing so many sad stories. The best advice I ever heard, however, was from my mentor and friend, J. William Worden who regularly reminded my colleagues and I in supervision to "trust the process."

When we know that most grieving people do find their way in a new life, it is much easier to observe their pain, knowing it will one day ease. These ideas will help you take care of yourself while you are taking care of others.

Keep Physically Fit. The stress of working with others is overwhelming at times, so make sure that you are eating a low-sugar, low-fat diet that includes a wide range of healthy foods. Exercise according to a plan worked out with your health professional and get plenty of rest.

Observe Faith Practices. Worship, scripture reading, and prayer are important practices to establish or enhance. Because work with grieving people involves grappling with issues of life and death, remaining spiritually fit is critical.

If you do not already have one, find a congregation where you connect with others and can find support and direction in your faith development. A member of the clergy or personal spiritual director can help you develop a plan for your own spiritual growth.

Whatever else leaders do, a life-long love of learning is an important value to practice

Love Learning. More than ever before, bountiful resources exist for bereavement support group leaders who want to continue learning. The Resource section at the end of this handbook is a starting point, as are the multitude of workshops and seminars available.

Local hospices, funeral providers, and hospitals often provide continuing education workshops, and CMI Education Institute (www.cmieducation.org) hosts regional workshops on a wide variety of bereavement-related topics.

Membership in the Association for Death Education and Counseling (www.adec.org) is also money well-spent. In addition to the association's bi-monthly newsletter filled with helpful articles, members can obtain discounted subscriptions to the leading journals in grief counseling: *Death Studies* and *Omega*. The association's annual spring conference affords an invaluable connection with colleagues who have shared interests.

Another avenue for learning is available through the online academic journal databases at your public library. From the comfort of your own home, you can access journals reporting all of the latest bereavement research and these services are generally free or available for a very nominal fee. Talk to the reference librarian to learn more about online database resources.

Get Supervision. One key to good work with bereaved people is gaining insight from more experienced bereavement group leaders. This "supervision" as it is called in clinical training programs, acknowledges that none of us has learned *everything* to be known about working with bereaved people.

Throughout my career, I have benefited from the expertise of colleagues who have different training and clinical experience than my own. Their fresh perspective has often helped me see things in my work I would never have otherwise seen. I think it is foolish to attempt to lead a bereavement group without the accountability of working with such a group or individual.

Real sadness sets in when a group fails to meet your expectations. Learn from the failures and keep trying!

The group mentioned in the introduction, led by J. William Worden, has been just such a group for me, contributing immeasurably to my professional growth for more than a dozen years. This group meeting on the second Wednesday of each month was so important to me that one week I flew home from the east coast on Tuesday night after speaking for a conference. I attended the Wednesday morning meeting with these colleagues and then flew back to the east coast on Wednesday night to speak on Thursday. I hope you will find a supervision group that will contribute so much to your growth that you will fly twice across the country to be there!

Bereavement groups do sometimes fail. Real sadness sets in when you have envisioned a bereavement group for weeks or months that fails to meet your expectation. But just because one group does not rise to your expectation does not mean you are destined to lead mediocre groups. Learn what you can from the shortcomings and work to avoid the errors that might have contributed to a group's failure. The dividends reaped from your investment in the lives of grieving people will be well worth the effort.

✎ Epilogue ✎

You have embarked on a unique journey. Whether you are a veteran support group leader or are just beginning to consider whether or not you should lead a group, I hope that you now realize that you can do it. Developing a group for bereaved people is a special calling.

While grief is a very personal experience with many features unique to a particular individual, the process of bereavement is not easily resolved alone. Humans are social beings; from time immemorial, people have derived support from each other. Bereavement support groups become caring communities of people who have experienced similar losses and are on a "journey" together to find healing and wholeness.

While you are on this journey, I trust that the principles here will guide you in your work. The resources in the following pages will help you as you learn to be a more effective group leader. You will find reproducible handouts for group meetings, a sample promotional flyer, and an annotated resource list of books to help you continue learning.

You might want to reproduce some of the pages in this section. If you are the purchaser of this handbook, you are granted permission to reproduce pages from the following section for your personal use in leading bereavement groups. The pages that can be legally copied include a permission statement at the bottom in case you use the services of a commercial copy center. Remember, though, that this handbook is protected by applicable copyright laws, so any other reproduction requires written permission from the publisher.

Thank you for learning how to be effectively involved in the lives of bereaved people. May you derive great joy and satisfaction as you live out your calling of *Guiding People Through Grief.*

My Reflections. . .

_____
_____
_____
_____
_____
_____
_____
_____
_____
_____
_____
_____
_____
_____
_____
_____
_____
_____
_____
_____
_____
_____
_____
_____

Finding Pathways Through Grief
A New Bereavement Community

Whether it was the death of your life mate, a close friend, or some other special relationship, grief is meant to be shared. Since everyone's experience with grief is somewhat unique, you won't find us telling you how you *ought* to grieve. Instead, what you will find here are friends who care—and understand—what you *are* going through.

Finding Pathways Through Grief is a mutual help support group. The group is not psychotherapy but it will help you navigate the difficulties of this new experience. No one has to talk but everyone is encouraged to. Each week, we will discuss the issues and concerns common to newly bereaved people, including. . .

- *What to make of the anger, discouragement, and guilt experienced in grief*
- *How to deal with the unfair expectations of other people*
- *Where to look for people you can trust to help you*
- *How to manage the holidays and other special occasions in grief*
- *Who to consider for additional support if you need it*
- *How to take care of yourself physically*

Monday afternoons beginning September 7

1:00 – 2:30 PM

Central Senior Center
1612 Main Street
Centerville

For more information, call Marci Dunn,
Educational Program Coordinator at 783-3232

Sadness is a normal response to a significant loss. The fatigue, sleep disruption, loss of appetite, inability to focus or concentrate, and an overall lack of drive are common experiences for people who have suffered a major loss. Most of this "reactive depression" lifts during the early months of bereavement. Care with the following will help minimize the effects of this reactive depression and will help you feel better even if you are coping with clinical depression (which should be diagnosed by a competent professional).

- *Eat a low sugar diet.* Sugar can contribute to the high one moment, low the next that complicates the emotional experiences of bereavement

- *Live a balanced life.* Bereaved people often try to fill every moment with activity; create some "white space" to think, reminisce, look at photos, and be sad.

- *Exercise regularly.* Make sure you talk to your healthcare professional about exercise, but regular habits of physical activity contribute to overall feelings of well-being

- *Connect with supportive people.* Whether through family relationships, a support group, or very good friends, make sure you are connected to people; no one grieves well alone.

- *Cultivate faith.* Worship, prayer, reading, and meditation all contribute to emotional well-being; don't neglect the practices that are so important in sustaining your spirit

- *Choose meaningful activity.* Even when you don't particularly feel like it, find some meaningful ways to give yourself to others. Volunteer and give yourself away.

- *Sleep regularly.* Most bereaved people have difficulty sleeping. Keep a journal and write down the things you are thinking about when you can't sleep. You might be surprised at how much better you sleep when you eat right, exercise regularly, and create "margin" in your life. Establishing a routine during the last hour or two before bed (journaling, warm bath, lower room lighting, soft music, prayer/meditation, etc.) can be very helpful in getting to sleep and staying asleep.

- *Talk through the loss.* You don't have to talk about the death to get through grief, but being able to discuss the experiences with a caring friend, family member, caregiving professional, or support group can be very helpful in reconciling the loss.

Even though no medication erases the sadness of loss or shortens the grief process, in limited cases, a physician may prescribe antidepressant medication. By all means, talk with your healthcare professional about the purpose of the medication, how it works, and what side effects are possible, as well as any other questions you have about depression and its treatment.

The following books make excellent reading. Though some of these books are out of print, copies can still be found in used bookstores and on the internet.

As you read, you will have to be patient with yourself. Most bereaved people have limited ability to concentrate. You might find it takes you much longer to read a book than before the loss. Try reading a chapter or a few pages every day or two. If you need to re-read a section a few times, do it.

You can increase the usefulness of the book if each time you complete reading a few pages, you stop and write in your journal. These questions might help you to reflect on what you're reading:

- What did I take away from these pages?
- What one idea I can practice in my own grief?
- What do I disagree with that the author said?
- How is this author really writing my story, almost as if she is looking over my shoulder?

Here are some books other bereaved people have found helpful. . .

- *How to Go On Living When Someone You Love Dies* by Therese A. Rando (general grief)

- *Midlife Orphan* by Jane Brooks (adult child's death of parent)

- *The Bereaved Parent* by Harriet Sarnoff Schiff (classic for parents after a child's death)

- *Widowed* by Joyce Brothers (popular psychologist reflects on what she has learned as a widow)

- *The Grieving Child* by Helen Fitzgerald (resources for parents on how to help children)

- *A Grace Disguised* by Jerry Sittser (how author coped when wife, mother, and daughter were all killed in an accident)

- *The Grieving Teen* by Helen Fitzgerald (help both for teenagers and those who care about them)

- *A Grief Observed* by C. S. Lewis (Christian philosopher's "journal" after his wife's death)

One of the ways parents and other caregivers can be supportive to grieving children is by reading books with them. While you may want to browse at your favorite bookstore to find available titles, here are some that other grieving parents, counselors, and educators have found useful.

- *When Dinosaurs Die: A Guide to Understanding Death.* by Laurie Krasny Brown and Marc Brown (ages 4-7)

- *When Someone Very Special Dies.* by Marge Heegaard (ages 6-11)

- *Lifetimes: The Beautiful Way to Explain Death to Children* by Bryan Mellonie and Robert Ingpen (ages 6-11)

- *Aarvy Aardvark Finds Hope* by Donna O'Toole (ages 6-11)

- *Cemetery Quilt* by Kent Ross, Alice Ross, and Rosanne Kaloustian (ages 6-9)

- *It Must Hurt a Lot* by Doris Sanford (ages 6-9)

- *Good-Bye, Vivi!* by Antonie Schneider and Maja Duskiova (ages 6-9)

- *Saying Good-bye to Grandma* by Jane Resh Thomas and Marsha Sewall (ages 6-11)

- *Fears, Doubts, Blues, and Pouts: Handling Fear, Worry, Sadness, and Anger* by Norman Wright. (ages 4-8)

- *Saying Goodbye to Daddy* by Judith Vigna (ages 6-8)

As you work through the grief process, you will find keeping a diary or journal to be helpful. In ancient times, rulers often used scribes to keep a careful record of what transpired in the king's life. Throughout history, thoughtful people have written down the important facts, places, and events of their lives—sometimes even publishing those journal entries in books to share with their families.

Journal-keeping in bereavement provides a couple of key benefits. Keeping a diary of your grief process helps you to organize your thoughts and feelings. If everything seems jumbled in your head, you will likely find that keeping a journal helps you make sense of "the jumble." Writing down your thoughts and feelings, as well as keeping a record of events, helps create order in the chaos.

In a few months, you will want to see the progress you have made in the grief process, and keeping a journal also provides this important benefit. Looking back at what you are writing now will provide an important yardstick and you will be able to see just how far you have come.

Any blank book will do—whether it is a leather-bound book printed on fine paper with gold edged pages or simply a spiral notebook you pick up at the discount store. Make sure you put a date on each entry, and even make an appointment with yourself to write at the same time every day or every week.

As you write, work to record more than events. Try to write a paragraph or two about what you *thought* and *felt* as you experienced the event. In other words, do not just write down that you went to the restaurant the two of you always frequented; write about what that was like, how was it different this time, and what you most missed about him or her sharing that time with you.

As you write, you will often get "stuck," unsure of what to write about. Here are some ideas to get you started in your journal. . .

- Today, I missed you the most when. . .
- I tend to feel the most (lonely/sad/angry/guilty/etc.) when. . .
- I wish that I would have. . .
- The events coming up that I most dread are. . .
- I need to say thank you to. . . for . . .
- What I am having the most difficulty making sense out of is. . .
- The things that remind me most often of you are. . .
- The dumbest things people have said to me are. . .
- The people who have been most supportive to me are. . .and what they have done to help is. . .

Dealing With Anger
in Your Grief

Managing anger is one of the hardest tasks facing people in bereavement. But like all the other emotions, anger is a natural part of the grief process for most people. On its own, anger is not a destructive emotion, but it can become harmful when we refuse to acknowledge it and deny its existence. Anger also becomes harmful when we express it in ways that are harmful to ourselves or others, destructive to property, and damaging of relationships.

Remember that anger sometimes serves a helpful purpose by motivating a person to take action. Many of the great reform movements of history were begun by people who were frustrated and angry about the way things were. *Mothers Against Drunk Driving* is just one example of such a movement, begun by Candace Lightner after her teenage daughter's death at the hands of a repeat-offending drunk driver. Here are some constructive ways to manage anger. . .

* write a letter in your journal to the person or experience that most evokes your anger

* keep an "anger diary" in which you record your experiences; each time you feel anger growing in your "gut," jot down what you're feeling, what thoughts or things led up to this moment, and what you did that helped the anger subside (how did you express it?). Later, you can evaluate whether you expressed it in a healthy way or not

* find a supportive friend, pastor, or counselor. Tell this person, "Right now I'm feeling angry. I think _____ is where the anger is coming from" or "I'm not even sure what I'm mad at. Will you ask me some questions to help me figure it out?"

* read scripture, attend worship, and pray

* exercise at the gym. Cardiovascular fitness can help stabilize emotions, but talk to your doctor first.

* practice deep breathing or relaxation techniques

* take a warm bath with candlelight (no artificial light) while breathing deeply and slowly

* take a brisk walk around the block (if your health allows and your doctor approves)

* avoid making major decisions when you are feeling intense anger

Managing the Expectations
of Others

An old adage says, "Free advice is worth about what you pay for it!" You have probably already noticed how many people have no shortage of advice for their friends in grief. You may have been told that what you need to do is *sell* your home or that what you need to do is *not sell* your home. You might have already received lots of ideas about how other people coped with their losses: "I just stayed busy," or "I didn't stay home for the holidays," or "I went right back to work so I wouldn't think about it."

You have likely also heard people suggest—sometimes quietly and sometimes aggressively— they know the best ways for you to cope: "You've just got to pull yourself together," or "She wouldn't want you carrying on like this," or "You've got to think about the children," or "What you need is a long vacation away from here."

♦ What is the "dumbest" thing anyone has said to you so far?

♦ What do you wish you had the courage to say to all of those people dispensing free advice?

♦ Why do you think the expectations of others have such an impact on us in bereavement?

Our lives have been turned upside down by this loss. We weren't sure we could get through it—and sometimes, we still wonder if we will. But together we have learned that expressing emotion is okay, that making new friends is essential, that wondering about faith is normal. We have grown.

Now, as we leave this place and this group, we acknowledge that we are different people. We still have far to go on this journey through grief. But overall, we are changed people with new tools and resources for the road ahead. We could never forget the ways our lives have been touched and changed by these people through whose deaths we have been thrust into the dark night of grief. Their memories provide joy and comfort even though they often bring us to tears.

It won't always be easy, but with God's guidance and the patient compassion of family and friends, we are confident we will grow through our grief. After the harsh cold and dark of winter, we will feel the warm glow of love in our lives and we will burst forth in full bloom again, welcoming the spring of new life. From this place, we go forth on the grief journey, confident that even though sorrowing, we are not without hope.

The future is filled with new people and experiences to cherish. Like a tiny plant poking its head through the remnants of the last winter snow, we will stretch into the warm sunshine of spring, burst forth in radiant color, and live fully again.

Reading and Internet Resources

An important element to success in leading bereavement groups is the continuing education you receive by attending workshops and reading books. While there are literally thousands of books about death and bereavement currently available, the ones listed here are absolutely the "best of the best!" These are the books in my library I find myself reaching for again and again.

Understanding Bereavement

Grief Counseling and Grief Therapy: A Handbook for the Mental Health Practitioner by J. William Worden (Springer, 2002). Now in its third edition, this is the definitive text for helping grieving people, even available in multiple languages. This volume details the four tasks of mourning for which Worden has become so widely known, and has much to teach anyone helping people in grief—mental health practitioner or volunteer.

How To Go On Living When Someone You Love Dies by Therese A. Rando (Bantam Doubleday, 1988). This useful book is an excellent resource, both for the group leader and for the person in grief. Dr. Rando explains many of the disturbing experiences of bereavement, helping the bereaved and their caregivers understand the process. Though most people in early grief have difficulty concentrating enough to read long books, this book's organization make it easy to find help fast.

The Anatomy of Bereavement by Beverly Raphael (Basic Books, 1983). This overview of bereavement from a developmental perspective is one of the best contributions to the field from this well-respected Australian clinician and researcher. Raphael's chapter on grief after a traumatic death is filled with practical insight.

Treatment of Complicated Mourning by Therese A. Rando (Research Press, 1993). This lengthy discussion of factors complicating bereavement is a helpful resource, though it is doubtful very many will read through the 750 pages in a single sitting. One value of Rando's professional books is the thorough overview of theories she provides, creating almost an "anthology" of the field.

Grief—The Mourning After: Dealing With Adult Bereavement by Catherine M. Sanders (John Wiley, 2001). This book is the culmination of three decades of research, which included development of the *Grief Experience Inventory (GEI)*, one of the most widely-used instruments for studying the effects of grief. From her research and clinical experience, the late Dr. Sanders outlines five phases of bereavement: shock, awareness of the loss, conservation-withdrawal, healing, and renewal. Her survey includes chapters on the personality, age, social, and family variables as well as practical ideas for dealing with complicated grief.

Bereavement: Counseling the Grieving Throughout the Life Cycle by David A. Crenshaw (Crossroad, 1996). A quick read, this book introduces the need to grieve throughout life and then provides reference points for the major stages of human development: preschool, school-age, adolescence, young adulthood, middle adulthood, and older adulthood.

Stories to Read With Children

When Dinosaurs Die: A Guide to Understanding Death. by Laurie Krasny Brown and Marc Brown (Little Brown, 1996). With wonderful illustrations, this book explains in simple terms many of the words children hear when someone dies and illustrates some of the reasons people (depicted as dinosaurs) die. The book offers a perspective on different cultural and religious beliefs and points children to their parents, teachers, and clergy as resources to help them explore their questions.

When Someone Very Special Dies. by Marge Heegaard (Woodland Press, 1988). This was one of the first workbooks for grieving children and is designed to help them learn about and better express the experiences of grief. Through the author's systematic approach, children learn that what they are feeling is normal and where they can turn for help. She sensitively helps children deal with matters of faith, anger, guilt, sadness, and fear while remembering the relationship they enjoyed with the person who died.

Lifetimes: The Beautiful Way to Explain Death to Children by Bryan Mellonie and Robert Ingpen (Bantam, 1983). Through beautiful art, the author and illustrator depict the lives of various plants and animals. This book shows how death is an inevitable part of life—even for people.

Aarvy Aardvark Finds Hope by Donna O'Toole (Compassion Books, 1988). This charming story recounts the experience of Aarvy who grieves the loss of his mom and sister after they are removed from their homeland to a zoo in another country. Aarvy's experiences of sadness and loss of appetite parallel those of many people in grief. He even gets angry with his friend, Ralphy Rabbit who tries to help. A teaching guide is also available and the story is available on VHS videocassette.

Cemetery Quilt by Kent Ross, Alice Ross, and Rosanne Kaloustian (Houghton Mifflin, 1993). Josie doesn't want to attend her grandfather's funeral at first, but she changes her mind when she learns about a family heirloom called the cemetery quilt. The quilt has little caskets added each time there is a death in the family. Though initially upset, Josie comes to feel comfort from knowing that death offers families a way to affirm the continuity of life.

It Must Hurt a Lot by Doris Sanford (Multnomah Press, 1986). When Joshua's dog, Muffin, is killed by a car, he must learn to make sense of "his world" without Muffin. He slowly begins to understand his emotions and the "big changes" that are coming about in him. Little by little, Joshua learns that loving means hurting and that friends want to help even when they don't know how. Since pet death is so common in childhood, this is a great book for the young elementary classroom.

Good-Bye, Vivi! by Antonie Schneider and Maja Duskiova (North-South Books, 1998). When Molly and Will's grandmother comes to live with them, she brings along her cherished canary, Vivi. Though

Vivi soon becomes an important member of the family, she gets sick and dies. Granny helps the children talk about their loss and come to terms with Vivi's death by remembering together how she had brightened their lives. Her words and model for the children at Vivi's death serve them well again when Granny dies and they find solace in her words and the memories of things she did.

Saying Good-bye to Grandma by Jane Resh Thomas and Marsha Sewall (Clarion, 1988). When Suzie's grandmother dies, her family drives a long way back to the town where her parents grew up. Throughout the next few days, Suzie learns about grief and funerals in this well-told story of love, remembering, and family. Each part of the funeral—visitation, service, burial, and post-funeral meal—are explained with details that answer many children's questions about this mysterious time.

Saying Goodbye to Daddy by Judith Vigna (Albert Whitman & Co., 1991). Clare must deal with the sudden death of her father in an automobile crash. Even though she is frightened, lonely, and angry, she is helped through the grieving process by her mom and grandfather. In the weeks after the funeral, she learns to remember her dad's funny way of saving everything and the other stories they share together as a family.

Helping Children and Teens

Children and Grief: When a Parent Dies by J. William Worden (Guilford Press, 1996). This book brings a great deal of clarity to the issues most often faced by children and teens after a parent's death. Based on his work in the Harvard Child Bereavement Study, you will find many practical ideas here.

Life and Loss: A Guide to Help Grieving Children by Linda Goldman (Routledge, 1999). Filled with ideas for engaging children in grief-support activities, this is one of the most practical "idea banks" you'll ever find for leading bereavement groups for children.

Fire In My Heart, Ice In My Veins by Enid Samuel Traisman (Centering, 1992.) This thought-provoking book is actually a journal and activity book for teens in grief. It provides ample space to record thoughts and feelings while guiding the adolescent to deal with anger, guilt, fear, regrets, sadness, and a host of other grief-related emotions.

The Grieving Child: A Guide for Parents by Helen Fitzgerald (Simon & Schuster, 1992.) One of the most practical resources for parents and professionals alike, this book provides helpful information in a question/answer format. Fitzgerald addresses trauma situations (like explaining suicide to children), funeral attendance, and developmental concepts of death. She shares a multitude of practical strategies.

Helping Teens Work Through Grief by Mary Kelly Perscy (Routledge, 2002). Using Worden's four tasks of mourning, Perschy develops a very workable approach to bereaved teens. This book is filled with activity ideas, group administration helps, discussion starters, and other resources. The second edition is now available but the first edition (©1997) is just as useful.

The Grieving Teen: A Guide for Teenagers and Their Friends by Helen Fitzgerald (Simon & Schuster, 2000). This is one of the best books for teens and those who care for them. Fitzgerald has used the stories of teens to help teens, and the author's creative numbering and cross-referencing of sections makes it easy for a teen to quickly find what he or she needs at the moment. With each of the 111 topics Fitzgerald treats, she offers a section entitled "What You Can Do" that provides practical, useful ideas.

Breaking the Silence: A Guide to Help Children With Complicated Grief by Linda Goldman (Brunner-Routledge, 2001). Considering several of the complicated losses children face—suicide, homicide, abuse, bullying, and AIDS among them—Linda Goldman provides practical guidance for educators, clincians, and all others called on to help children.

Child and Pregnancy Loss

The Bereaved Parent by Harriet Sarnoff Schiff (Penguin, 1977). In a very readable 146 pages, the author helps parents in grief find their way through bereavement back to "the land of the living." She addresses issues of the funeral, guilt, powerlessness, marriage, religion, and a dozen other issues. About this book, Elisabeth Kubler-Ross wrote, "It does not make death beautiful, it does not console in an unrealistic way—but it tells the truth—and is very reassuring and helpful because of it."

Miscarriage: Women Sharing From the Heart by Marie Allen and Shelly Marks (John Wiley, 1993). These two psychotherapists who personally suffered miscarriages use this book to report their study of more than 100 mothers living through the same loss. The book is filled with insight and the appendix includes practical suggestions for a variety of caregivers including mental health professionals, clergy, and physicians. Support group leaders will better understand prenatal loss through this book.

A Silent Sorrow/Pregnancy Loss: Guidance and Support for You and Your Family by Ingrid Kohn and Perry-Lynn Moffitt (Bantam Doubleday Dell, 1992). While written for bereaved parents, this book has much to teach professionals and volunteers who provide care for them. The book deals with miscarriage, ectopic pregnancy, stillbirth, and medically-necessary abortions as well as the different aspects of the loss experienced by moms and dads, grandparents, and other children in the home.

Empty Arms by Pam Vredevelt (Multnomah, 1994). Written from a Christian perspective, this is a very personal account of the author's loss of an almost full-term stillborn baby. She sensitively touches many subjects, including how husbands and wives grieve differently. She also offers practical suggestions for building memories and dealing with the reactions of others.

Pastoral Care in Bereavement

All Our Losses, All Our Griefs by Kenneth R. Mitchell and Herbert Anderson (Westminster John Knox Press, 1983). This is one of the best books around to guide pastors and lay pastoral caregivers in understanding and ministering to bereaved people. The authors describe the grief process and how it intersects with theology. They also provide helpful, practical advice for leading funerals and memorial gatherings.

Grief, Transition, and Loss by Wayne E. Oates (Augsburg Fortress, 1997). A revised classic in the field, Oates offers much practical wisdom about the grief process. This is a good psychologically-oriented approach that makes application to pastoral care.

When Faith is Tested: Pastoral Responses to Suffering and Tragic Death by Jeffry Zurheide (Augsburg Fortress, 1997). Relying heavily on the theology of Karl Barth, Zurheide has crafted a masterful approach to ministering to people when unspeakable losses occur. This book is must-reading for anyone in pastoral care called upon to help someone when death makes no sense.

A Grace Disguised: How the Soul Grows Through Loss by Jerry Sittser (Zondervan, 2004). In 1991, college professor Sittser was driving his family's vehicle when they were involved in a head-on crash with a drunk driver, killing Sittser's wife, mother, and four-year old daughter. Written a few years after that horrific day, he reflects on what it was like to become a widower and single father to their three surviving, traumatized children while trying to cope with unimaginable sorrow.

Grief and Growth: Pastoral Resources for Emotional and Spiritual Growth by R. Scott Sullender (Paulist, 1985). Grief is not just something to endure; it is an opportunity for emotional and spiritual growth, Dr. Sullender says. Among other opportunities he discusses is the chance for the recovering bereaved to become helpers to newer bereaved individuals.

Facing Death Together: Parish Funerals by Margaret Smith (Liturgy Training Publications, 1998). Written by an Australian religious sister, this book provides practical insights on every aspect of the Catholic Church's bereavement and funeral ministry. Her perspective on the meaning behind the liturgical elements is quite helpful for bereavement volunteers. Though the focus here is on the funeral ministry, this will be immensely helpful for support group leaders who are not familiar with the meanings behind Roman Catholic funeral customs.

Sacred Sorrow: Reaching Out to God in the Lost Language of Lament by Michael Card (NavPress, 2005). From the pen of this contemporary Christian songwriter comes this exceptional analysis of the biblical genre of lament. Examining David, Jeremiah, Job, and Jesus, Card has created an outstanding book for helping pastoral caregivers understand sorrow. This is also good reading for those who are experiencing illness, grief, and loss.

Group Leadership Strategies

The Theory and Practice of Group Psychotherapy by Irvin D. Yalom and Mollie Leszcz (Basic Books, 2005). Now in its fifth edition, this book is a classic in group leadership. While the authors are addressing therapeutic groups led by mental health professionals, their insights on dealing with difficult group member personalities alone are worth the price of the book! They also address transference issues for group leaders and how to effectively screen participants, along with a wide diversity of other topics related to group leadership.

Effective Support Groups by James E. Miller (Willowgreen, 1998). This book provides a wealth of practical guidance in a very short, readable format.

Self-Help and Support Groups: A Handbook for Practitioners by Linda Farris Kurtz (Sage, 1997). This resource book discusses similarities between different models of groups and illustrates the principles with a wide variety of support group and self-help group models.

Group Work: Strategies for Strengthening Resiliency edited by Timothy Kelly, Toby Berman-Rossi, and Susanne Palambo (Haworth Press, 2001) Well-researched and written from a social work perspective, here is a collection of practical articles dealing with such issues as developing communities, helping group members grow in resiliency, and dealing with psychological problems in group work.

Websites and Organizations of Interest

The Compassionate Friends (international group of bereaved parents and siblings with national and regional conferences as well as local chapters)   www.compassionatefriends.org

American Association of Suicidology (research and support materials for families, professionals and volunteers who support people bereaved after a loved one's suicide)   www.suicidology.org

The SIDS Alliance (regional and national organization with resources related to Sudden Infant Death Syndrome)   www.sidsalliance.org

AARP Grief and Loss Program (resources from the American Association for Retired Persons, with access both for members and non-members)   www.aarp.org/griefandloss

National Hospice and Palliative Care Organization (resources related to hospice, end of life care, and bereavement)   www.nhpco.org

National Alliance for Grieving Children (provides links to children's grief support programs across the country, conferences, and resources)   www.nationalallianceforgrievingchildren.org

Association for Death Education and Counseling (international association of professionals and volunteers)   www.adec.org

American Academy of Bereavement/CMI Education (provider of regional workshops and other resources specifically related to bereavement and end-of-life care)   www.cmieducation.org